Legal Ethics for Lawyers: A New Model demonstrates how an Aristo-Kantian model of theoretical legal ethics could address the moral vacuum created by the dominant positivist model of legal ethics and professional conduct rules. Dr Mescher is to be commended bringing a fresh and insightful perspective to the debate.

Professor Joan Loughrey, *Professor of Law, School of Law, Queens University, Belfast, Northern Ireland*

Legal Ethics for Lawyers: A New Model is an excellent study of a vitally important issue. The author develops a genuinely original model of legal ethics based on Aristo-Kantian principles to replace the prevailing positivist model and applies it to concrete cases. No-one concerned with legal ethics can ignore this book.

Dr David Wood, *Principal Fellow, Melbourne Law School, Melbourne, Australia*

Barbara Mescher's *Legal Ethics for Lawyers: A New Model* draws on Kant and Aristotle to develop a compelling practical legal ethics. It will be invaluable to all lawyers looking to go beyond narrow, positivist approaches to professional obligations.

Dr Hugh Breakey, *Deputy Director, Institute for Ethics, Governance, and Law and Senior Research Fellow, Moral, Legal, and Political Philosophy, Griffith University, Brisbane, Australia*

Legal Ethics for Lawyers

This book proposes a new model of legal ethics.. This model will enable lawyers to advise clients upon both the law and ethics. This will better protect clients, and society, and enhance lawyers' professional obligations. The current model of legal ethics developed in the 19th century has two limbs: theoretical legal ethics that specified the role of lawyers was only to interpret the law, not also to give ethical advice. The second limb concerns lawyers' professional obligations. The present model of legal ethics no longer reflects the needs of modern legal practice. Now lawyers' professionalism is underpinned by greater demands from clients and society for the inclusion of ethical principles in legal practice and advice.

This book draws on moral philosophy to present a new model of legal ethics that explains the analytical process to include ethical advice. It analyses the potential harm of the present model to the legal profession, who have duties to the law and justice that may compete with demands by clients to serve them. Further, lawyers' professional duty to clients to act in their best interests is sometimes not adequately fulfilled as legal ethics does not permit lawyers to give ethical advice even if it may be in clients' best interests to do so. This book includes a detailed case study of corporate law practice to show why a new legal ethics is required. Other case examples are provided to demonstrate that lawyers practising in all areas of law encounter ethical issues and they too will benefit from a new legal ethics. The book will be essential reading for lawyers, professional bodies, academics, and students.

Dr Barbara Mescher is a lecturer at the University of Sydney, Australia, in significant areas for business and the professions, including securities regulation, corporate governance, and professional ethics. Barbara previously worked as a corporate lawyer and has continued to engage with the legal profession over several years as a member of the profession's Corporate Lawyers' Committee and the Ethics Committee.

Routledge Research in Legal Philosophy

Procedural Justice and Relational Theory
Empirical, Philosophical, and Legal Perspectives
Edited by Denise Meyerson, Catriona Mackenzie, and Therese MacDermott

The Origin of Copyright
Expression as Knowing in Being and Copyright Onto-Epistemology
Wenwei GUAN

Constitutional Imaginaries
A Theory of European Societal Constitutionalism
Jiří Přibáň

Human Dignity and the Law
A Personalist Theory
Michał Rupniewski

Legal Ethics for Lawyers: A New Model
A New Model
Barbara Mescher

For more information about this series, please visit:
https://www.routledge.com/Routledge-Research-in-Legal-Philosophy/book
-series/RRLP

Legal Ethics for Lawyers
A New Model

Barbara Mescher

Routledge
Taylor & Francis Group

LONDON AND NEW YORK

First published 2023
by Routledge
4 Park Square, Milton Park, Abingdon, Oxon OX14 4RN

and by Routledge
605 Third Avenue, New York, NY 10158

Routledge is an imprint of the Taylor & Francis Group, an informa business

© 2023 Barbara Mescher

British Library Cataloguing-in-Publication Data
A catalogue record for this book is available from the British Library

Library of Congress Cataloging-in-Publication Data
Names: Mescher, Barbara, author.
Title: Legal ethics for lawyers : a new model / Barbara Mescher.
Description: Abingdon, Oxon [UK] ; New York, NY : Routledge, 2022. |
Series: Routledge research in legal philosophy | Includes bibliographical references and index. |
Identifiers: LCCN 2022030625 | ISBN 9781032205892 (hardback) |
ISBN 9781032206097 (paperback) | ISBN 9781003264286 (ebook)
Subjects: LCSH: Legal ethics. | Attorney and client. | Ethics. | Law--Philosophy.
Classification: LCC K123 .M47 2022 | DDC 174/.3--dc23/eng/20220831
LC record available at https://lccn.loc.gov/2022030625

ISBN: 978-1-032-20589-2 (hbk)
ISBN: 978-1-032-20609-7 (pbk)
ISBN: 978-1-003-26428-6 (ebk)

DOI: 10.4324/9781003264286

Typeset in Times New Roman
by Deanta Global Publishing Services, Chennai, India

Contents

Acronyms and Abbreviations   ix

1 Introduction   1

Overview   1
Creating a New Moral TLE Model   2
Significance of This Book   3
Conclusion   5

2 Lawyers and Their Clients   6

Lawyers' Professional Obligations   6
Behavioural Ethics   13
Corporate Lawyers and Their Clients   14
Conclusion   19

3 The James Hardie Case Study   20

James Hardie's Asbestos Tort Liability   20
External Lawyers and the Restructure   27
JHIL's ASX Disclosure Obligation   32
Court Approval of JHIL's Restructure   36
MRCF Funding Shortfall   41
James Hardie's New Funding Arrangement   44
Conclusion   45

4 Theoretical Legal Ethics: Positivist v Moral Principles 47

The Role of Lawyers   48
The Law and Ethics   53

Client Supremacy   60
The James Hardie Case and Positivist TLE   63
Conclusion   66

5 Legal Ethics and Moral Philosophy   68

An Overview of Three Moral Philosophies   68
The Moral Philosophy of Aristotle   69
The Moral Philosophy of Immanuel Kant   73
Conclusion   76

6 Lawyers' Professional Obligations and Moral Philosophies   78

Lawyers' Professional Integrity   78
Lawyers' Duties to the Law and Justice   84
Lawyers and Clients: Fiduciary and Confidentiality
*   Duties   88*
Lawyers' Practical Wisdom and Judgement   91
Conclusion   95

7 A New Model of Legal Ethics   96

Core Principles of a Moral TLE   96
Steps in a Moral TLE (summary)   97
Cognitive Processes and Legal Practice   98
Step I: Moral Sensitivity   101
Step II: Moral Reasoning and Practical Wisdom   103
Apply Steps I and II to James Hardie's Lawyers   107
Step III: Dialogue with Clients   112
Conclusion   115

8 Conclusion   117

Legal Ethics and Legal Practice   118
The Role of Moral Philosophy   120
The Originality of the New Legal Ethics Model   121
Significance of the New Legal Ethics Model   122

Index   125

Acronyms and Abbreviations

The James Hardie Case Study

ABN 60	ABN 60 Pty Ltd, shell company – after the 2001 restructure of JHIL
Allens	Allens Arthur Robinson, Solicitors
Amaba	Amaba Pty Ltd
Amaca	Amaca Pty Ltd
ASIC	Australian Securities and Investments Commission, corporate regulator
ASX	Australian Securities Exchange
Jackson Report	'Special Commission of Inquiry into the Medical and Compensation Foundation' (Report, September 2004) David Jackson QC, Commissioner
JH	The James Hardie group
JHIL	James Hardie Industries Ltd, parent company of James Hardie group prior to 2001 restructure
JHI NV	James Hardie Industries NV, the group's new parent company – following the 2001 restructure
Macdonald case	*Australian Securities and Investments Commission v Macdonald (No 11)* [2009] NSWSC 287
MRCF	Medical Research and Compensation Foundation
Scheme/Restructure	Scheme of Arrangement
TLE	Theoretical Legal Ethics
Trowbridge	Trowbridge Deloitte Limited, actuaries

Person, Role/Position

Cameron	Peter, Solicitor, Senior Partner, Allens; Director, JHI NV August 2003–January 2006
Edwards	Sir Llewellyn, Managing Director, MRCF, Director, JHIL August 1990–February 2001

Jackson	David F, Commissioner, Special Commission of Inquiry into the Medical Research and Compensation Foundation
Macdonald	Peter, Managing Director, Chief Executive Officer, JHIL November 1999–January 2002; Director and Chief Executive Officer, JHI NV August 2001–October 2004
Morley	Phillip, Chief Financial Officer, JHIL, March 1997–October 2001; Director, James Hardie Coy Ltd and Jsekarb Pty Ltd, February 1997–February 2001
O'Meally	John Lawrence, Judge, NSW Court of Appeal
Robb	David, Solicitor, Partner, Allens
Santow	Kim, Judge, Supreme Court of NSW
Shafron	Peter, General Counsel, JHIL and the James Hardie group March 1997–November 1998; Company Secretary, JHIL, November 1998–March 2002

1 Introduction

This book analyses the effect of a positivist theoretical legal ethics (TLE) on a fundamental area of legal practice: lawyers' professional independence.

- Positivist TLE supports client supremacy requiring lawyers to adhere to clients' wishes to the extent that lawyers' independence is diminished. This has consequences for lawyers' professional obligations, as follows.
- Lawyers' fiduciary duty to clients relies upon lawyers' professional independence to enable them to give objective advice.
- Lawyers' duty to the law and to justice are core duties whose foundation is professional independence.
- Positivist TLE, therefore, affects lawyers' independence and ability to engage fully in the responsibilities of professional practice.

Overview

This book presents a new model of legal ethics, one with moral principles. The purpose of legal ethics is to guide lawyers' conduct in the daily practice of law and in their relationship with clients. There are two limbs in legal ethics. The first, positivist TLE, provides principles and values. The present model of TLE is based upon a positivist philosophy and it specifies a narrow role for lawyers: to interpret the law without recourse to ethical issues. The second limb refers to lawyers' professional obligations along with conduct rules, in the common law and statute. Both limbs of legal ethics are closely connected.

Problems with positivist TLE undermine lawyers' professionalism and their ability to meet society's ethical and legal expectations in the 21st century. The role of legal ethics is to safeguard lawyers' professional integrity, upon which clients and community trust are based, yet positivist TLE is detrimental to this role. This is a serious problem for the legal profession. This

DOI: 10.4324/9781003264286-1

book provides a new model of TLE informed by moral principles which complement and enhance lawyers' professional obligations.

The role of lawyers is restricted to the interpretation of the law without ethical considerations. This has created an ethical vacuum for lawyers, yet questions about lawyers' ethical obligations arise constantly, for example in the 2008 global financial crisis. Positivist TLE says that ethical concerns are not lawyers' responsibility. The need for ethical advice arises from ethical issues in clients' instructions, or an unethical use to which legal advice is put by clients. This failure of positivist TLE impacts the professionalism of lawyers who then may be perceived by clients as acting as legal service providers, rather than as professionals making independent judgements. The reason clients seek legal opinion is that they trust lawyers to give independent advice, but positivist TLE is a barrier to this. This affects lawyers' fiduciary duty, which relies upon lawyers giving independent and objective advice in the clients' best interests.

Lawyers' most important duties are to the law and justice. These take priority over duties owed to clients. Lawyers' independent assessment of these public duties is at the core of their professional obligations. Positivist TLE may, according to researchers, require lawyers to 'participate in injustice'.[1] Lawyers may believe they are not adequately serving their clients because of their loss of independence. This may create psychological issues for lawyers as they understand that their professionalism is not meeting their own expectations.

In the James Hardie (JH) case study (Chapter 3) some legal advice was used by clients to make decisions with a widespread negative impact upon direct stakeholders and the community. The external lawyers-to-client relationship was analysed regarding JH's legal and ethical issues as well as professional issues created by positivist TLE.

Creating a New Moral TLE Model

The new moral TLE relies upon the moral philosophies of Aristotle and Kant. Lawyers are not philosophers, but the new model is framed to enable lawyers to apply it in legal practice. This model envisages that lawyers give both ethical and legal advice to clients. Lawyers, therefore, will have an additional role to that of being only interpreters of the law, under positivist TLE. They will also learn how to identify ethical issues in clients' instructions and give ethical advice.

---

1 William Simon, *The Practice of Justice: A Theory of Lawyers' Ethics* (Harvard University Press, 1998) 2.

There are three analytical steps in this model. Step I concerns moral sensitivity and its acquisition. Step II is about moral reasoning and practical wisdom and how one engages in it. Step III guides lawyers in their dialogue with clients, where lawyers explain their advice. This new model, with its infusion of ethics, will provide greater moral content for lawyers and this will enrich both limbs of legal ethics: professional obligations and theoretical legal ethics. The beneficiaries of this reform are the legal profession, clients, and the public good.

The new model is designed to overcome the elements of positivist TLE that affect lawyers' professionalism: namely, the lack of ethics in positivist TLE. The new model provides lawyers with additional protection that is important to them both professionally and personally:

- This model will assist lawyers to uphold their duties to the law and justice by increasing their professional independence to permit objective assessment of the facts. Ethical analysis will further clarify potential legal issues.
- The new model will negate another adverse effect upon lawyers personally. This is where positivist TLE, without a focus upon ethics, leads lawyers to 'more often do things they believe to be unjust' and so sacrifice their personal moral autonomy.[2] Moral principles in TLE will return lawyers' moral autonomy.
- Lawyers' fiduciary duty to act in the best interests of clients will now include ethical matters as it is argued this broader scope *is* in the best interests of clients.
- An Australian study revealed other consequences for lawyers' legal practice.[3] There was 'a remarkably high level of self-reported stress and negative emotional states' and there were 'concerns about the structure and culture of legal practice'.[4] The new model alerts lawyers to stress factors identified by behavioural ethics and how to deal with them.

Significance of This Book

The book argues for true ethics in lawyers' TLE and presents a new and morally robust model informed by the moral philosophies of Aristotle and

---

2 William Simon, 'Authoritarian Legal Ethics: Bradley Wendel and the Positivist Turn' (2012) 90(3) *Texas Law Review* 709, 726.

3 Janet Chan, Suzanne Poynton and Jasmin Bruce, 'Lawyering Stresses and Work Culture: an Australian Study' (2014) 37(3) *University of New South Wales Law Journal* 1062.

4 Ibid., 1063.

Kant to assist transactional lawyers when they advise clients. Scholars maintain that lawyers' advice needs to include matters of moral responsibility.[5] This is an important professional issue for lawyers, as failure to give ethical advice could contribute to both lawyers and clients being in breach of the law.

An example is lawyers' advice to the Catholic Church in relation to victims of abuse. The Church opted for secrecy instead of considering their ethical position.[6] The client needed to assist victims of abuse and there was also an opportunity for the client to protect its reputation.[7] In this case a positivist TLE contributed to the lawyers' breach of the law because they had breached their fiduciary duty to the client by not advising that the client's best interest was to honour its duty to its parishioners.

Another example is the JH case study (Chapter 3). Here there were many unaddressed ethical issues that could not be part of lawyers' advice due to the narrowness of positivist TLE. The case showed the legal and ethical impact of positivist TLE upon the client and lawyers' decisions. Lawyers may reasonably argue: 'I am not an ethicist and, therefore, need not give ethical advice', yet here it was demonstrated as being a short-sighted view. Clients' decisions that are predicated upon lawyers' advice *do* matter. If these decisions are closely linked to lawyers' advice, then there may be adverse legal and professional implications for lawyers.

The principles of TLE have a vital role in legal practice, hence the significance of this book for the legal profession. Lawyers' professional obligations more generally are guided by TLE which has a holistic influence. The TLE principles mediate and provide a mode for ethical influence upon empirical situations encountered in legal practice. Positivist TLE, centred upon the law, is unable to be an ethical influence.

The new moral TLE changes the role of lawyers to one that is informed by the law and morals. This gives all lawyers a new and valuable social role as gatekeepers. Here, lawyers will be able to advise clients that there are alternative paths to achieve their commercial and other goals without offending the law or ethics.

The book exposes a paradox of positivist TLE. Its primary focus is upon the law resulting in legal advice failing to consider ethics. This could encourage clients to believe that their lawyers' non-inclusion of ethical

5 Tony Foley, 'Institutional Responses to Child Sexual Abuse: How a Moral Conversation with its Lawyers Might Contribute to Cultural Change in a Faith-Based Institution' (2015) 18(2) *Legal Ethics* 164, 180.

6 Robert K Vischer, 'Legal Advice as Moral Perspective' (2006) 19(1) *Georgetown Journal of Legal Ethics* 225, 230.

7 Ibid.

issues in their advice is either lawyers' acquiescence to clients' decisions or lawyers' underdeveloped morality as professionals.[8] These perceptions potentially harm the entire profession and its perceived and actual integrity.

Another paradox is that while seemingly characterised as singularly about the law and what is legal, positivist TLE may increase the possibility of immoral and sometimes illegal acts by clients (and occasionally, their legal advisors). This occurs in a climate where ultimately the clients' single-minded pursuit of different goals, for example, greater profit, predominates, despite of (or ignorant of) an increased risk of stakeholder harms and consequent reputational damage being sustained by both clients and lawyers.

Conclusion

The book, therefore, is not just about bringing moral principles into lawyers' TLE. It also explains why this is so important to the legal profession, and to the social contract that lawyers have with society to act for the public good. Much is at stake for the whole legal profession if it continues to support positivist TLE. It is outdated when one considers the legal and ethical environment in which lawyers practice today. Legal ethics is an important part of all lawyers' mode of professional practice. It is a matter of professional (and personal) integrity that lawyers are professionally permitted to address ethical issues. Moral philosophy will invigorate legal ethics.

Chapter 2 examines lawyers' professional obligations and conduct rules, including positivist TLE. Chapter 2 introduces external law firms, corporate lawyers, and the tension within their relationship with corporate clients whose in-house lawyers instruct the law firm. This is a necessary prelude to the JH case study in Chapter 3. It assists in understanding the lawyer-to-client relationship. Although this case study concerns corporate law practice, the case is an example of the effects of positivist TLE upon lawyers and clients in all areas of legal practice.

---

8 Laura P Hartman, Joseph DesJardins, and Chris MacDonald, (McGraw Hill Irwin, 5th ed., 2021) 45–50.

2 Lawyers and Their Clients

Chapter 2 examines the second limb of legal ethics, lawyers' professional obligations, and conduct rules, including professional integrity, independence, duties to the law and justice, fiduciary duty, and the public good. The first limb of legal ethics, theoretical legal ethics (TLE), is summarised in this chapter as it influences lawyers' professional practice and their professional obligations. It is important to appreciate there is ethical content in lawyers' professional obligations and to contrast this with lawyers' TLE whose focus is the law.

Chapter 2 also introduces law firm corporate lawyers and the tension in their relationship with corporate clients whose in-house lawyers instruct law firms. We need to understand the lawyer-to-client relationship in corporate law practice. This analysis gives a context for the James Hardie case study in Chapter 3.

Lawyers' Professional Obligations

Historically, professions had a strong ethical imperative as members saw themselves as responding to a '*calling* ... measured primarily in *moral* terms'.[1] This may explain the inclusion of ethical principles in lawyers' professional obligations. Clients too, rely upon ethical concepts to engage with lawyers as they trust in their lawyers' expertise. Professionals above everyone else, are trusted to apply their expertise for an appropriate purpose.[2] This is where the significance of professional integrity is most apparent.[3]

---

1 Max Weber, *The Protestant Ethic and the Spirit of Capitalism* (Talcott Parsons trans., Unwin University Books, 1930) 79–80 (emphasis in original).
2 Sir Daryl Dawson, 'The Legal Services Market' (1996) 5 *Journal of Judicial Administration* 147, 48–9.
3 Stan van Hooft, *Understanding Virtue Ethics* (Acumen, 2006) 162.

DOI: 10.4324/9781003264286-2

Competence and uniformly high standards, requiring 'an inner consistency between deed and principle'[4] is the essence of integrity. Lawyers' professional obligations also include legally binding duties to the law and justice;[5] and to clients – fiduciary[6] and confidentiality duties.[7] Further, there is the practical wisdom and judgement lawyers use to advise clients.

The first limb of legal ethics, TLE, also began with moral terms as the interpretation of law had to be compatible with the 'higher standards of morality'.[8] This changed in the 19th century when law was regarded as having the moral neutrality of science.[9] Therefore, TLE was unlike the second limb, where moral terms were retained. The consequence is that the two limbs of legal ethics are ethically opposed. This places lawyers' commitment to ethical conduct entirely upon their professional obligations. The new moral model of TLE will bring symmetry to the two limbs of legal ethics.

Independence

Professional independence involves the exercise of judgement 'in accordance with community standards of competence and ethicality'.[10] Usually, lawyers enjoy autonomy in relation to their clients. Lawyers derive their power vis-á-vis clients from the fact that as professionals they are independent. Professional autonomy is the 'key to the integrity of professional practice and work', being 'relative or absolute freedom from external authority and having the privilege of peer or self-supervision'.[11] This freedom is 'one of the foundations upon which professions base their claim to autonomy'.[12]

Professional independence permits members of the professions to make appropriate judgements across a range of matters, including acting within

---

4 David Luban, 'Integrity: Its Causes and Cures' (2003) 73 *Fordham Law Review* 279, 279.

5 G E Dal Pont, *Lawyers' Professional Responsibility* (Lawbook Co, 2021) 567.

6 Paul D Finn, *Fiduciary Obligations* (Law Book, 1977).

7 *Legal Profession Uniform Law Act 2014* (NSW) s423(2)(b)(i).

8 Augusto Zimmermann, *Western Legal Theory, Concepts and Perspectives* (LexisNexis Butterworths, 2013) 82.

9 Ibid., 66.

10 Emma Oakley and Steven Vaughan, 'In Dependence: the Paradox of Professional Independence and Taking Seriously the Vulnerabilities of Lawyers in Large Corporate Law Firms' (2019) 46(1) *Journal of Law and Society* 83, 88.

11 Joan Bagust, 'The Legal Profession and the Business of Law' (2013) 35(1) *Sydney Law Review* 27, 28 (emphasis added).

12 Richard L Abel, 'Comparative Sociology of Legal Professions' in Richard L Abel and Philip P Lewis (eds), *Lawyers in Society, vol 3, Comparative Theories* (University of California Press, 1989) 80, 133.

professional ethical standards and in the public good. The new moral model of TLE envisages lawyers asserting their professional independence and taking the role of ethical 'gatekeeper',[13] identifying ethical issues, then advising clients against ethical misconduct.[14]

Expertise

In the usual lawyer-to-client relationship, lawyers, unlike their clients, have expertise in the law, and this contributes to lawyers' power. In Australia lawyers typically undertake five years of university study: a law degree combined with another undergraduate degree with a further six months studying the practical legal process. The lawyers' professional body requires those with a practising certificate to regularly update their knowledge.[15] Expertise, is a core professional ideal leading to monopoly power where professions exercise 'economic power and control over the market for their services'.[16]

Expertise creates 'certain duties and responsibilities' that professionals owe their clients.[17] Further, 'ethics is the way' ... [that] 'the moral duty of specialists comes into being',[18] yet this is inconsistent with a positivist TLE. Society rewards professionals' unique knowledge and competence 'in esoteric bodies of knowledge linked to central needs and values of the social system'.[19]

Law and Justice

Lawyers have a professional 'duty to obey and uphold the law'[20] and 'a responsibility to be cognizant of law's purposive and ethical intent'.[21]

---

13 Justine Rogers, Dimity Kingsford Smith, and John Chellew, 'The Large Professional Service Firm: A New Force in the Regulative Bargain' (2017) 40(1) *University of New South Wales Law Journal* 218, 221.

14 Ibid.

15 Law Society of NSW, Continuing Professional Development Programme (CPD) requires the completion of ten CPD units per year: https://www.lawsociety.com.au/CPD

16 Ysaiah Ross, *Ethics in Law: Lawyers' Responsibility and Accountability in Australia* (LexisNexis, 5th ed, 2010) 60.

17 Vladimir Bakshtanovskii and Iurii Sogomonov, 'Professional Ethics: Sociological Perspectives' (2007) 46(1) *Sociological Research* 75, 76.

18 Ibid.

19 Magali Sarfatti Larson, *The Rise of Professionalism: A Sociological Analysis* (University of California Press, 1977) x.

20 Dal Pont, above n 5, 653.

21 Barbara Mescher, 'Lawyers' Professional Ethics: Where are the Ethics?' (2018) 34(1) *Journal of Professional Negligence* 21, 25.

Lawyers are custodians 'of the rule of law'[22] and involved in its development.[23] Their relationship with the law is 'reflexive in that lawyers constitute the law and are also constituted and regulated by it'.[24] Lawyers' role is to interpret the law that binds us all thus giving lawyers a more clearly defined part in acting in the public good.[25] Positivist TLE agrees with this but it is a superficial and narrow view of lawyers' role. The professional obligations go further and combine legal duties with ethical principles.

Lawyers have a duty to the administration of justice and are officers of the court.[26] The duties to the law and justice extend beyond the court, to include 'the performance by lawyers of any act in the course of' their legal practice,[27] including legal advice. These duties are immersed in the ethical ideals of fairness and honesty that are embedded in the law.[28] Lawyers are admitted to practise law by the Supreme Court and swear an oath of office to 'truly and honestly conduct myself in the practice of a barrister (or a solicitor) of the Supreme Court'.[29]

The law operationalises justice by its promotion, protection, and enforcement of individual private and public rights and in accordance with due process involving lawyers and the judiciary.[30] The role of lawyers is 'to promote justice and hence serve society'.[31] Legal practice includes a social and ethical role that satisfies society's need 'for a just, fair and efficient method of individuals understanding the rules and expectations of society'.[32]

22 Rogers, Kingsford Smith, and Chellew, above n 13, 224.
23 Donald Nicolson and Julian Webb, *Professional Legal Ethics: Critical Interrogations* (Oxford University Press, 1999) 1.
24 John Flood, 'The Re-Organization and Re-Professionalization of Large Law Firms in the 21st Century: From Patriarchy to Democracy' (2012) 36 *Journal of the Legal Profession* 415, 426.
25 James Allsop, 'Professionalism and Commercialism: Conflict or Harmony in Modern Legal Practice?' (2010) 84 *Australian Law Journal* 765, 773.
26 Dal Pont, above n 5, 569.
27 Dal Pont, above n 5, 570.
28 Geoffrey Hazard, 'Law and Justice in the Twenty-First Century' (2001) 70 *Fordham Law Review* 1739, 1740.
29 *Supreme Court Act 1970* (NSW); *Supreme Court Rules (Amendment No 244) 1990* (NSW) r 4.
30 Scott L Cummings, 'Introduction: What Good are Lawyers?' in Scott L Cummings (ed.), *The Paradox of Professionalism: Lawyers and the Possibility of Justice* (Cambridge University Press, 2011) 1, 15.
31 Nicolson and Webb, above n 23, 1; Cummings, ibid., 27.
32 Allsop, above n 25, 769.

Serving the Public Good

Lawyers have a significant social role to serve the public good as this provides the continuing justification of all professions.[33] The public good requires lawyers to be 'conscious of broader obligations than the minimums established by law',[34] especially when clients request legal advice upon proposed strategies having socially unacceptable objectives. However, lawyers' public service role has been substantially diminished as is evidenced by 'elite lawyers [having] mostly dropped the rhetoric of professional public-serving ideals'.[35] Serving the public good is closely aligned with ethics as 'morality can only be thought of as duties owed to *society at large*, to the common good'.[36]

Fiduciary Duty

Lawyers' fiduciary duty reflects the usual position of lawyer dominance and client vulnerability, this being the reason for lawyers to act in the clients' best interests.[37] The underlying assumption here is that lawyers' expertise and influence constitute a position of power vis-á-vis clients who are regarded as vulnerable to any abuse of power by their lawyers[38] acting against clients' interests. Lawyers are 'not simply agents of clients',[39] rather, they use their expertise and independence to identify clients' best interests.

The 'fiduciary obligation is the strictest known to our legal system'.[40] It derives from the common law[41] and statute.[42] It is also an *ethical* principle,[43]

33 Richard Moorhead, 'Precarious Professionalism: Some Empirical and Behavioural Perspectives on Lawyers' (2014) 67 *Current Legal Problems* 447, 450–1.

34 Deborah Rhode, 'Personal Integrity and Professional Ethics' in Kieran Tranter et al. (eds), *Reaffirming Legal Ethics: Taking Stock and New Ideas* (Routledge, 2010) 28, 39 (emphasis in original).

35 Robert Gordon, 'Portrait of a Profession in Paralysis' (2002) 54 *Stanford Law Review* 1427, 1443.

36 Roger Cotterrell, *Emile Durkheim: Law in a Moral Domain* (Edinburgh University Press, 1999) 55 (emphasis in original).

37 Finn, above n 6.

38 *Hospital Products Ltd v United States Surgical Corp* (1984) 156 CLR 41.

39 Robert Gordon, 'A New Role for Lawyers? The Corporate Counsellor after Enron' (2003) 35 *Connecticut Law Review* 1185, 1200, (emphasis added).

40 Allsop, above n 25, 772.

41 *Hospital Products Ltd v United States Surgical Corp* (1984) 156 CLR 41.

42 *Legal Profession Uniform Law Act 2014* (NSW) s 423(2)(b) and *Legal Profession Uniform Law Australian Solicitors' Conduct Rules 2015* (NSW) r 4.1.1.

43 Paul D Finn, 'The Fiduciary Principle' in Timothy G Youdan (ed.), *Equity, Fiduciaries and Trusts* (Toronto, 1989) 1, 55 (emphasis in original).

one that reflects the ethical duty of moral philosopher Kant, to assist vulnerable others.[44] Mason J applied the 'power and vulnerability' principle in *Hospital Products Ltd v United States Surgical Corporation*,[45] a test that is now widely used in Australia.[46]

> The relationship between the parties is therefore one which gives the fiduciary a special opportunity to exercise the power or discretion to the detriment of that other person who is accordingly vulnerable to abuse by the fiduciary of his position.[47]

Fiduciary principles or maxims originate in equity and are also drawn from ethics. The maxim, 'equity acts on the conscience', is an ethical principle and ethics is also in this maxim: equity looks to 'that as done which *ought* to be done'.[48] The fiduciary role as a protector of another's interests, is both legal in equity, and *'ethical'*.[49] The role relies upon ethical principles of honesty, integrity, and lawyers' professional judgement, ideals that are also consistent with fundamental principles of moral philosophy.[50]

Legal Ethics

It is essential that professionals realise the ethical dimensions of their role as 'we rely upon them for the truth' and they 'often serve as the collective conscience for the rest of us'.[51] Ethics is so important to the professional endeavour that 'the observance of ethical guidelines and enforcement of ethical principles' are 'the essence of a profession'.[52] It is a concern, therefore, that this is not reflected in the first limb of legal ethics, positivist TLE, although there are ethical principles in the second limb of legal ethics, the professional obligations, as indicated above.

---

44 Nicolson and Webb, above n 23, 15.
45 (1984) 156 CLR 41, (High Court).
46 Paul D Finn, 'Fiduciary Reflections' (2014) 88 *Australian Law Journal* 127, 136.
47 *Hospital Products Ltd v United States Surgical Corp* (1984) 156 CLR 41, at 96–7.
48 John Burke, *Osborn's Concise Law Dictionary,* (Sweet & Maxwell, 6th ed., 1976) 134; Manuel Velasquez, *Business Ethics: Concepts and Cases* (Pearson Prentice Hall, 6th ed., 2006) 10–12.
49 Finn, above n 43, 55 (emphasis in original).
50 Mary Midgley, 'The Origin of Ethics' in Peter Singer (ed.), *A Companion to Ethics* (Blackwell, 1993) 5.
51 Clancy Martin, Wayne Vaught, and Robert Solomon, *Ethics Across the Professions: A Reader for Professional Ethics* (Oxford University Press, 2010) 2.
52 Allsop, above n 25, 767.

Theoretical Legal Ethics

Positivist TLE keeps ethics at the periphery of the role of lawyers. This removes the support ethical ideals could give lawyers to help counter conflicts of interest and to better meet their professional obligations. Clients may use lawyers' advice to make unethical decisions and say these decisions flow from their lawyers' legal advice. It is not simply enough to bring morals per se into TLE; a structured model is needed. The new moral TLE provides this structure, and the moral philosophies lawyers require to identify and advise upon ethical issues in clients' instructions and strategies.

Statutory Legal Ethics

Statutory legal ethics supports lawyers' professional integrity and legal professional standards to ensure 'lawyers are competent and maintain high ethical and professional standards in the provision of legal services'.[53] Lawyers must 'ensure appropriate safeguards are in place for maintaining the integrity of legal services'.[54] Lawyers also have a professional statutory duty to maintain their reputation and that of the legal profession.[55] There are similar provisions in other Australian states and territories.[56]

Professional Bodies' Statement of Ethics

Solicitors' professional bodies, the Law Societies in every state, each has a Statement of Ethics[57] as a source of legal ethics. This is a conduct guide for lawyers that includes legal obligations and ethical aspirations such as honesty. Solicitors are expected to display this statement in their offices for the benefit of clients. The 'purpose of such codes is without doubt to persuade the public that the formulation of ethical standards justifies their trust'.[58] Others question codes saying they are 'a means of collective self-deception' and 'for social scientists to confuse those prescriptions with

---

53 *Legal Profession Uniform Law Act 2014* (NSW) s 3(b).

54 Ibid., s126(a).

55 *Legal Profession Uniform Law Act 2014* (NSW). *Legal Profession Uniform Law Australian Solicitors' Conduct Rules 2015,* r 5.1; 5.1.1 and 5.1.2 Dishonest and Disreputable Conduct.

56 https://www.lawcouncil.ann.au/policy-agenda/regulation-of-the-profession-and-ethics/australian-solicitors-conduct-rules

57 Law Society of NSW, *Statement of Ethics* https://www.lawsociety.com.au/practising-law-in-NSW/ethics-and-compliance/ethics/statement+of+ethics

58 Eliot Freidson, *Professionalism: The Third Logic* (University of Chicago Press, 2001) 214.

actual behaviour would display unpardonable naivete'.[59] Both views have some merit. The codes are there to persuade the public but also to inspire lawyers. The codes are not about self-deception, rather, 'ethics' needs to be understood by lawyers in the context of legal practice. This is the function of ethics in the new moral TLE.

Behavioural Ethics

Any discussion of ethical decision-making and advising requires acknowledgement of behavioural ethics to assist us in understanding other factors influencing our decisions. Researchers reveal that human beings share a delusion concerning their own ethicality.[60] We have 'ethical blind spots' where there is a 'gap between how ethical we think we are and how ethical we truly are'.[61] This delusion is sustained by our prediction 'that we will behave as we think we *should* behave, but at the time of the decision, we behave how we *want* to behave'.[62] There is always the possibility that what we want to do *is* what we should do. In addition, our recall may also be deluded, as when we recall our earlier decisions we tend to 'reinterpret our unethical behaviour as ethical'.[63] We think 'that we acted as we thought we *should* behave'.[64] Psychologically, we need a self-perception that we behave ethically and we are 'good, worthwhile individuals'.[65]

Behavioural ethics tells us that awareness will assist us to address the delusion of ethicality. Lawyers need to know that this delusion relates to our two systems of thinking. System one, less considered thinking, contributes to the delusion and is more likely to be unethical, but system two, reflective and reasoned thinking, is more suitable for complex decisions.[66] If we are aware of the delusion of ethicality, we can address it by consciously engaging in system two thinking to take us 'toward the ideal image we hold of ourselves'.[67]

59 Richard L Abel and Philip S C Lewis, 'Putting Law Back into Sociology of Lawyers' in Richard L Abel and Philip S C Lewis (eds) *Lawyers in Society, vol 3, Comparative Theories* (University of California Press, 1989) 281, 495.

60 Max H Bazerman and Ann E Tenbrunsel, *Blind Spots: Why We Fail to Do What's Right and What to Do About It* (Princeton University Press, 2011).

61 Ibid., 1.

62 Ibid., 153 (emphasis in original).

63 Ibid., 159.

64 Ibid., 153 (emphasis in original).

65 Donald Langevoort, 'Where Were the Lawyers? A Behavioral Inquiry into Lawyers' Responsibility for Clients' Fraud' (1993) 48 *Vanderbilt Law Review* 75, 103.

66 Bazerman and Tenbrunsel, above n 60, 153–4.

67 Ibid., 154

Corporate Lawyers and Their Clients

Corporate lawyers advise major businesses either from within as in-house lawyers, or as external lawyers in major law firms. These lawyers constitute 20 per cent of practising lawyers, not a majority,[68] but their impact exceeds their numbers[69] due to the nature of their clients and how they use lawyers' advice. For example, some decisions of Australia's largest banks and financial institutions adversely affected hundreds of thousands of stakeholders and were the subject of an Australian Government Royal Commission in 2019.[70] The 2008 global financial crisis shows that these issues arise in many countries. In the UK, the Solicitors Regulation Authority (SRA) engaged researchers to study the professional challenges in the corporate lawyer-to-client relationship.[71]

Corporate clients are often public listed companies, usually parent companies within a group of subsidiary proprietary companies. Eighty-nine per cent of Australia's top 500 listed companies have 'at least one controlled entity' (subsidiary).[72] There are good reasons for this as a large commercial enterprise is easier to manage if its functions are spread across many companies in the group, each having a role in the overall business.[73]

A group structure can insulate 'the parent's assets from a liability that could arise' elsewhere in the group.[74] Company law treats each company as a separate entity,[75] irrespective of its group status. Each company has its

---

68 Law Society of NSW, *Practicing Solicitors Statistics* [as at 31 December 2019/2020] (2020) https://www.lawsociety.com.au/sites/default/files/2020-01/201912_Practising _Solicitor_Statistics-Dec.2019.pdf

69 Law Society of NSW, *NSW Profile of Solicitors 2016* (Final Report, 2017) 27. https://www .lawsociety.com.au/sites/default/files/2018-04/NSW_PROFILE_OF_SOLICITORS_2016 _FINAL_REPORT_pdf

70 Commonwealth, Royal Commission into 'Misconduct in the Banking, Superannuation and Financial Services Industry' (Final Report, 2019) Kenneth Maddison Hayne, AC, QC, Commissioner ('*Banking Royal Commission*') https://financialservices.royalcommission .gov.au

71 Claire Coe and Steven Vaughan, *In Dependence, Representation and Risk: An Empirical Exploration of the Management of Client Relationships by Large Law Firms* (Solicitors Regulation Authority, 2015). https://www.sra.org.uk/globalassets/documents/sra/research /independence-report.pdf?version=4a1ab7

72 Ian Ramsay and Geoff Stapledon, *Corporate Groups in Australia,* Research Report (Centre for Corporate Law and Securities Regulation, University of Melbourne, 1998) v http://cclsr .law.unimelb.edu.au

73 Robert Austin and Ian Ramsay, *Ford, Austin, and Ramsay's Principles of Corporations Law* (LexisNexis, 17th ed., 2018) [4.270] 160.

74 Ibid., [4.310] 163.

75 *Salomon v Salomon & Co Ltd* [1897] AC 22.

own legal obligations and makes decisions through its directors and officers who are its fiduciaries.[76]

In-House Corporate Lawyers

In-house and external lawyers are equal in all ways as professionals. Their differences relate to their institutional context. External lawyers are more independent than in-house lawyers due to their greater distance from the clients. It is advantageous for a company to employ its own lawyers to apply their legal expertise to the company's unique legal and business concerns. However, in-house corporate lawyers could be conflicted as employees of the client company. They are required to provide legal advice to achieve company goals. There is tension between the apparent 'capture' of in-house lawyers by their employer, their obligation to observe professional duties, and the need to assert professional independence.[77] Empirical research reveals that all in-house lawyers prioritise their obligations to their 'client' (the company that employs them) and that although this is understandable pragmatism it 'is not how their relevant professional codes of conduct see professional obligations'.[78]

General counsel are senior in-house lawyers and usually hold a practising certificate. Consequently, they have more professional obligations. General counsel may find their professional duties 'are often inconsistent with or irrelevant to the practical requirements of their work'.[79] Further, under company law, general counsel may also be designated as officers of the company, if, as is often the case, they participate in decisions affecting the company's business.[80] This makes senior counsel subject to directors' and officers' duties.[81] General counsel instruct external law firms on behalf of their company. A former Human Rights Commissioner has attributed an ethical role to both in-house and external lawyers:

> In-house counsel have become the moral conscience of the company or firm or government body for which they are working. Their

---

76 *Corporations Act 2001* (Cth) ss 180–4.
77 Richard Moorhead and Victoria Hinchly, 'Professional Minimalism? The Ethical Consciousness of Commercial Lawyers' (2015) 42(3) *Journal of Law and Society* 387, 390.
78 Richard Moorhead, Steven Vaughan and Cristina Godinho, *In-House Lawyers' Ethics: Institutional Logistics, Legal Risk and the Tournament of Influence* (Bloomsbury, 2019) 199.
79 Susan Hackett, 'Corporate Counsel and the Evolution of Ethical Practical Navigation: An Overview of the Changing Dynamics of Professional Responsibilities in In-House Practice' (2012) 25 *Georgetown Journal of Legal Ethics* 317, 319.
80 *Corporations Act 2001* (Cth) s 9.
81 Ibid., ss 180–4.

responsibility is not only to determine whether an action is strictly legal, but whether it will lead to an ethical outcome in the wider community. [82]

External Corporate Lawyers

External corporate lawyers are employed by large law firms whose extensive resources are needed by corporate clients to provide complex legal advice for matters such as corporate restructures and fundraising.[83] The work of these lawyers is important as they 'facilitate almost every [significant] economic activity and business transaction in society'.[84] External lawyers are instructed by the clients' in-house lawyers due to their knowledge of the company. Law firms provide a team of lawyers, each member being responsible only for specific legal issues. Structural fragmentation in the way law firms handle clients' matters has profound professional consequences. It may be difficult for these lawyers to be fully aware of and, therefore advise upon, possible 'risks to ethics and other professional standards'.[85] Corporate lawyers may find 'themselves functioning more and more under the control and direction of their powerful and savvy corporate clients',[86] as only they have all the facts.

Tensions arise when in-house lawyers have a different opinion from that of the external lawyers, on the law or clients' best legal strategy.[87] In-house lawyers' opinion is likely to be more favourable to clients' commercial strategies, yet external lawyers may perceive it as questionable law and perhaps a threat to the integrity of the legal system.[88] Corporate clients could use their power to define their own interests. This may override external lawyers' professional role as fiduciaries as they need to independently determine what is in their clients' best interests. However, positivist TLE

---

82 Gillian Triggs, 'In-House Counsel Should be Corporate World's "Moral Compass"', *Lawyers Weekly,* 5 March 2015. http://www.lawyersweekly.com.au/news

83 *Corporations Act 2001* (Cth) chs 6, 6D, 5.

84 Rogers, Kingsford Smith, and Chellew, above n 13, 219.

85 Christine Parker, Adrian Evans, Linda Haller, Suzanne Le Mire, 'The Ethical Infrastructure of Legal Practice in Larger Law Firms: Values, Policy and Behaviour' (2008) 31 *University of New South Wales Law Journal* 158, 163–5.

86 Bagust, above n 11, 52.

87 KPMG, *Through the Looking Glass: How Corporate Leaders View the General Counsel of Today and Tomorrow* (September 2016) 5 https://home.kpmg/au/en/home/insights/2016/08/through-the-looking-glass-general-counsel-report-2016.html

88 Christine Parker and Adrian Evans, *Inside Lawyers' Ethics* (Cambridge University Press, 3rd ed., 2018) 39.

requires lawyers to prioritise client demands[89] that may, paradoxically, work against clients' interests and cause lawyers to breach their fiduciary duty.

Three empirical studies were conducted in the UK where legal ethics comprised similar elements to Australia's positivist TLE.[90] In the first study researchers for the SRA examined lawyers' independence from clients in corporate finance law firms, specifically: 'how commercial and client pressure affect large firms and their lawyers' professionalism'.[91] Interviews were conducted with 53 senior partners from 20 of the world's largest law firms and their Compliance Officers for Legal Practice. The study found 'the lawyer-client relationship had become so entirely one-sided that professional independence, both in terms of autonomy and detached disinterested reflection, had indeed become a myth'.[92] Further, that partners rarely 'perceived a significant ethical conflict with a client; instead, they took on the moral outlook of their clients. As such their independence was a form of self-deception.'[93]

In the second study, 21 corporate lawyers were interviewed, comprising both external and in-house lawyers.[94] The study compared the responses of both groups for the purpose of determining how their professional 'ethical consciousness' is shaped.[95] The study found that both groups exhibited similar attitudes and that ethical consciousness was minimal.[96] This was attributed to the power and pragmatism of business as it challenged professional ethics.[97]

The third study was undertaken of 57 corporate lawyers in global law firms in the City of London who were asked how they would 'describe an ethical lawyer'.[98] Most said, those that complied 'with the law', and only 33 per cent said those who exhibited 'values or morality'.[99] This response

---

89 W Bradley Wendel, *Lawyers and Fidelity to Law* (Princeton University Press, 2010) 6.

90 Solicitors' Regulation Authority (SRA) United Kingdom; Competence Statement A, *Ethics Professionalism and Judgement,* A1 see https://www.sra.org.uk/solicitors/competence-statement.page

91 Coe and Vaughan, above n 71, 3.

92 Oakley and Vaughan, above n 10, 97.

93 Ibid., 101.

94 Moorhead and Hinchly, above n 77, 389.

95 Ibid., 387.

96 Ibid., 387–9.

97 Ibid., 387.

98 Steven Vaughan and Emma Oakley, '"Gorilla Exceptions" and the Ethically Apathetic Corporate Lawyer' (2016) 19 *Legal Ethics* 50, 58–9.

99 Ibid., 59.

reveals the consequence of adherence to positivist TLE where law is a priority and morality is at the periphery. [100]

External Lawyers' Conflicts of Interest

Law firms' financial self-interest may conflict with their professional obligations. Many major law firms depend financially upon corporate clients, as their fees comprise the firms' core income stream. Lawyers are under pressure to achieve maximum billable hours.[101] Understandably, firms are reluctant to put their relationship with these clients at risk. The consequences of this conflict affect professional duties to protect lawyers' independence and satisfy professional ethics.

Professional independence enables lawyers to make their own judgement regarding client instructions where the firm is expected to uphold the role of lawyers. This role makes lawyers trustees of the legal system with 'an overriding duty to maintain the justice and integrity of the legal system, even against client interests, in the public interest'.[102] However, there is a divergence of the 'commercial pressures of the firm from the ethical standards of professionalism'.[103] In addition, there is a conflict of interest when law firms reward corporate lawyers with bonuses for successful outcomes for clients. Yet, acting on the instructions of some clients may not be in the professional interests of either the lawyers or their firms.

These examples could also conflict with lawyers' statutory legal ethics obligation 'to ensure appropriate safeguards are in place for maintaining the integrity of legal services'[104] and the profession.[105] Integrity is difficult to maintain if lawyers endeavour to comply with clients' requests for a particular commercial outcome that may only be achieved if some lawyers assist clients in 'creative compliance' with the law.[106]

If conflicts for law firms and their corporate lawyers are unresolved it makes lawyers vulnerable to accusations that legal practice is at risk of becoming a business rather than a profession.[107] A key finding of the SRA

---

100 Dennis Lloyd, *The Idea of Law: A Repressive Evil or Social Necessity?* (Penguin Books, 1981) 111.

101 Flood, above n 24, 428.

102 Parker and Evans, above n 88, 39.

103 Flood, above n 24, 428.

104 *Legal Profession Uniform Law Act 2014* (NSW) s 126(a).

105 Ibid., s 423(2)(iv): the authority for the *Legal Profession Uniform Law Australian Solicitors' Conduct Rules 2015* (NSW) See rr 4, 5.

106 Parker and Evans, above n 88, 296.

107 Bagust, above n 11, 27.

report was that corporate clients use their contract with the law firm 'to reduce the distinctiveness' of corporate 'lawyers as legal professionals ... such that they are seen as, and perceive themselves to be, and begin to behave like, mere "service providers"'.[108]

This is a significant problem for corporate lawyers where conflicts of interest create 'tension between the pursuit of commercial advantage' by lawyers and their 'ethic of service to the client and public'.[109] Some major law firms have dealt with this matter by enabling a hybrid professional model:[110] one that is neither a business nor unequivocally a professional model.

Conclusion

Legal ethics across lawyers' professional obligations, codes, and statute is dominated by the influence of positivist TLE which reinforces clients' power and encourages lawyers' acquiescence. It is important in legal practice that there is an awareness by lawyers of ethical issues. Lawyers have a unique opportunity to deal with these matters. A new moral TLE would permit lawyers to take up this opportunity.

The legal and commercial cases company clients bring to corporate lawyers could affect hundreds of thousands of stakeholders: shareholders, employees, creditors, and, indirectly, consumers. Financial markets too are affected due to the large scale of some clients' business operations. Clients' instructions may pose ethical problems for corporate lawyers. A positivist TLE provides insufficient guidance and support to address these problems.

Chapter 3 analyses the James Hardie case study[111] and the external lawyer-to-client relationship. It shows many of the ethical issues faced by corporate lawyers and their effect upon lawyers' legal duties and professional responsibilities. It also reveals the sometimes-insidious role of positivist legal ethics that can contribute to lawyers and their clients breaching the law. The case study provides detailed specific examples of legally complex matters and the ethical issues flowing from them.

---

108 Coe and Vaughan, above n 71, 1.

109 James Spigelman, *Are Lawyers Lemons? Competition Principles and Professional Regulation* (2002) St James Ethics Centre, 29 October 2002. http://www.lawlink.nsw .gov.au

110 Rogers, Kingsford Smith, and Chellew, above n 13, 257.

111 New South Wales, Special Commission of Inquiry into the Medical Research and Compensation Foundation (Report, September 2004) David Jackson QC, Commissioner https://www.dpc.nsw.gov.au/publications/categories

3   The James Hardie Case Study

Chapter 3 examines the lawyer-to-client relationship between an external corporate law firm, Allens Arthur Robinson, Solicitors (Allens), and its client, James Hardie Industries Ltd (JHIL),[1] the subject of this case study and the centre of a major government-initiated public inquiry known as the *Jackson Inquiry*.[2] Many of the decisions of the lawyers and their client, JHIL, and the context in which they were made, are taken from this *Inquiry's* report (*Jackson Report*). Chapter 3 turns the lens of the argument to the corporate client, its commercial problems, its choice of strategies, and how ethical issues may arise. This is the context in which external lawyers are instructed by clients and the advice lawyers provide. Allens, as professionals, had to consider not only the client's strategies, but also the corporate law and its own professional duties, including legal ethics.

James Hardie's Asbestos Tort Liability

In 2001 the James Hardie (JH) group of companies comprised its parent company, JHIL, and 69 subsidiaries over which JHIL exercised control by owning either 'all the shares or, at least more than 50% of them'.[3] The group's profits had been made in Australia. These were later affected by asbestos-related tort liabilities requiring compensation payments to former employees of wholly owned subsidiaries Amaba Pty Ltd (Amaba) and Amaca Pty Ltd (Amaca): Australia's major asbestos mining and manufacturer of building products using asbestos.

---

1 NB see Table of Contents, Appendix, for abbreviations used in this chapter.
2 New South Wales, 'Special Commission of Inquiry into the Medical Research and Compensation Foundation' (Report, September 2004) David Jackson QC, Commissioner ('*Jackson Report'*) [1.6] 8. https://www.dpc.nsw.gov.au/publications/categories
3 Harry Glasbeek, 'Contortions of Corporate Law: James Hardie Reveals Cracks in Liberal Law's Armour' (2012) 27 *Australian Journal of Corporate Law* 132, 135.

DOI: 10.4324/9781003264286-3

Employers have a duty of care in the tort of negligence to provide a safe system of work for employees.[4] The duty relates to foreseeable risks.[5] It was alleged that substantial investors and managers in the JH companies, had known since 1935, that 'asbestos was a killer'.[6] Indeed 'asbestosis was common in the 1920s and 1930s'.[7] The link between asbestos and mesothelioma was made in 1960,[8] although it took until the late 1980s before JH's 'asbestos operations had been ... wound down'.[9] Employers also have long-standing statutory duties to ensure 'the health of workers and the conditions of the workplace are monitored for the purpose of preventing illness and injury of workers arising from the conduct of [that] business'.[10] There were doubts about the degree to which JH companies discharged these duties.[11]

Calculating Tort Liability

The first negligence claims for compensation made against JH companies arose prior to the late 1970s. The legal issue of negligence also highlighted ethical concerns that lawyers could have addressed in their advice if they had had a different model of theoretical legal ethics (TLE).

Tort victims were those employees of Amaba and Amaca who had already been diagnosed with asbestos-related illness. Future claimants were former employees and members of the public such as tradesmen or home renovators, yet to be diagnosed, who had come into contact unknowingly with JH products containing asbestos.

The board of JHIL engaged Trowbridge Deloitte Limited (Trowbridge) to provide professional actuarial assessments to assist JH group and its parent company, JHIL, calculate its future asbestos tort liability. The Trowbridge 1996 and 1998 reports[12] showed the potential future liability for the group was increasing, with the 1996 report estimating a liability of A\$230 million, and the 1998 report estimating A\$254 million.[13] These tort claims grew

---

4 *Wilson and Clyde Coal Co Ltd v English* [1938] AC 57
5 *Donoghue v Stevenson* [1932] AC 562.
6 Ian Verrender, 'Hardie's legal marathon ends with statement of the bleeding obvious'; and 'The shameful legacy of James Hardie', *Sydney Morning Herald,* 5 May 2012 https://www .smh.com.au
7 *Jackson Report,* above n 2, [2.6] 18, footnote 4.
8 Ibid., [2.6], 18, footnote 4.
9 Glasbeek, above n 3, 138.
10 *Work Health and Safety Act* (NSW) 2011, s 19(3)(g).
11 *James Hardie & Co Pty Ltd v Hall as administrator of Estate of Putt* (1998) 43 NSWLR 554, 576–7; *Briggs v James Hardie & Co Pty Ltd and others* (1989) 16 NSWLR 549.
12 *Jackson Report,* above n 2, [15.1] 201.
13 Ibid., [2.12–2.13] 20.

rapidly. Amaca had paid claimants A$18.3 million for the 12 months to 31 March 2000 and expected to pay A$37 million for the 15 months to 30 June 2001.[14]

A Trowbridge report was undertaken for the year 2000. Unfortunately, it was incomplete.[15] Figures for the asbestos claims from 1 April to 30 December 2000 were absent, a time when claims were accelerating from A$20.3 million in 2000 to an anticipated A$30 million in 2001.[16] A 'key assumption underlying the Trowbridge 2000 Report' was that mesothelioma had peaked, yet (the then) 'current data suggested that the assumption may have been wrong (as indeed it was)'.[17] Later, JHIL maintained that Trowbridge had indicated it (Trowbridge) did not need this missing data, although Trowbridge claimed it had requested the data from JHIL who declined to provide it.[18] Therefore, Trowbridge's report to the board in February 2001 (the restructure meeting, see below), did not calibrate the effect of the recent claims experience.[19] Commissioner Jackson accepted JHIL's statement[20] but noted that JHIL directors should have been aware that current data was required.[21]

Actuarial reports do have limitations that are exacerbated if not properly prepared. The Commissioner found that Trowbridge's February 2001 report was prepared without due care and diligence because its assessment was a 'projection of future liabilities [that] significantly understated the position' and may not have met the requisite standard.[22] The Commissioner also found that the report was possibly misleading as it gave a 'distinctly optimistic' estimate.[23] Peter Shafron, JHIL's in-house corporate lawyer and group counsel, advised in October 2000 that he thought the liability estimates in the Trowbridge reports 'very imperfect'.[24]

Commissioner Jackson concluded that it appeared no member of the board, including JHIL's managing director, had read any of the Trowbridge assessments.[25] However, the board did have access to more reliable

---

14 Ibid., [26.1], 459.
15 Ibid., [24.2] 391.
16 Ibid., [24.71] 416.
17 Ibid., [24.68] 415.
18 Ibid., [24.4] 391.
19 Ibid., [26.41] 472.
20 Ibid., [24.16] 396.
21 Ibid., [24.66] 414.
22 Ibid., [23.1] 373.
23 Ibid., [23.15] 378; [23.6]–[23.8] 374–5, especially [23.7]; [23.9] 375.
24 Ibid., [24.65] 413.
25 Ibid., [15.3] 201.

information in that it had a 'quarterly report on asbestos litigation' that revealed this had increased significantly along with substantial settlements.[26]

This unsatisfactory situation reveals that JHIL's liability calculations could have been affected by Trowbridge's negligence and the lack of attention by JHIL to the incomplete nature of the reports. Directors have a common law duty of care to inform themselves of the financial position of their company,[27] and a statutory duty of care.[28]

There was an historical example for JHIL to use to calculate its tort liabilities. Johns-Manville Corporation (Manville) was a US company experiencing extensive asbestos tort liabilities. Manville was 'the largest manufacturer and largest supplier of asbestos products' in the US[29] but by 1982 'three cases per hour, every hour' each business day were being filed against it.[30] Manville estimated its liability at this time to be over US$1 billion.[31] It decided on a company reorganisation whereby a trust was created to pay tort claimants. However, the asset pool was so small that after 20 years Manville's claimants received only 5 per cent of their entitlements.[32]

Manville and JHIL could have addressed the risks of asbestos tort claims many years before by protecting their workers. This would have been the ethical thing to do. Instead, they chose to retain – for the company and shareholders – the profits from asbestos. The companies' long delay in honouring their legal duty of care obligations meant that the number of claims substantially increased, creating a massive tort liability that could not be fully met, effectively denying adequate compensation to those who had produced their profits.

Separate Legal Entity

It was vital for JHIL, as parent company in the JH group, to establish whether it could be liable for the tort liabilities of its subsidiaries, Amaba and Amaca. This was a legal question involving the doctrine of a company's separate legal entity and the principle of limited liability. These permit each

---

26 Gideon Haigh, *Asbestos House: The Secret History of James Hardie Industries* (Scribe Publications, 2006) 268.

27 *Daniels (formerly practicing as Deloitte Haskins & Sells) v Anderson* (1995) 37 NSWLR 438, 500.

28 *Corporations Act* (Cth) *2001* s 180.

29 Peta Spender, 'Blue Asbestos and Golden Eggs: Evaluating Bankruptcy and Class Actions as Just Responses to Mass Tort Liability' (2003) 25 *Sydney Law Review* 233, 226.

30 Ibid., 227.

31 Ibid.

32 Ibid., 253.

company as a separate entity, to use only its own assets to compensate victims of its torts.[33] In order to make JHIL legally liable, claimants would have the difficult task of defeating both the legal doctrine of the separate legal entity and the limited liability principle, both entrenched in corporate law.[34] Nevertheless, JHIL had some foundation for its concern. It had already been a party to litigation where attempts were made to make it liable.[35]

In *James Hardie & Co Pty Ltd v Hall as Administrator of Estate of Putt*,[36] Putt had been an employee of one of the parent company subsidiaries in New Zealand, James Hardie & Co (NZ), (JH & Co NZ). The parent company, JHIL, had a shareholding of over 95 per cent in this company.[37] Putt was exposed to asbestos at work but was statute barred[38] from taking common law action against the NZ employer. He sought common law damages from related companies, the parent company, JHIL, and James Hardie and Co Pty Ltd, both registered in New South Wales (NSW). Putt argued that these companies supplied asbestos to his NZ employer.[39] Putt's claim could succeed if the separate legal entity status of the companies could be ignored. The legal issue was whether the NSW companies owed a duty of care to Putt, as Judge O'Meally at first instance, appeared to consider.[40] JH & Co NZ appealed this decision, and the Court of Appeal upheld the appeal. It found no evidence that the NZ company was a 'mere façade', being controlled by the NSW companies, but instead the NZ company was a separate entity, and *it* had a duty of care to Putt, rather than the NSW companies.[41]

The legal and practical reality of the Anglo-Australian law on limited liability was that by the time Putt's case was decided, it was virtually impossible that case law would result in JHIL, as parent company, being held liable to tort claimants formerly employed by its subsidiaries.

If there was any residual risk of JHIL, being liable, it would have arisen from the very slight factual possibility that JHIL had directed the asbestos processing subsidiaries, Amaba and Amaca. The direction had to be so close

---

33 Peta Spender, 'Second Michael Whincop Memorial Lecturer: Weapons of Mass Dispassion – James Hardie and Corporate Law' (2005) 14 *Griffith Law Review* 280, 285.

34 David Bennett, "Recent Peeks under the Corporate Veil" in David Chaikin and Gordon Hook (eds) *Corporate and Trust Structures: Legal and Illegal Dimensions* (Australian Scholarly, Melbourne, 2018) 49.

35 *James Hardie & Co Pty Ltd v Hall as administrator of Estate of Putt* (1998) 43 NSWLR 554; *Briggs v James Hardie & Co Pty Ltd and others* (1989) 16 NSWLR 549.

36 (1998) 43 NSWLR 554.

37 Ibid., 557.

38 *Accident Rehabilitation and Compensation Insurance Act (1992)* (NZ) s 17.

39 (1998) 43 NSWLR 554, 557.

40 Ibid., 581.

41 Ibid., 584.

that the three companies could be joint tortfeasors, each being liable to contribute: *CSR Ltd v Wren*.[42]

In *Briggs v James Hardie & Co Pty Ltd*[43] other arguments were used by the plaintiff. Briggs was a former employee of Asbestos Mines Pty Ltd (Asbestos), a subsidiary company owned by parent company JHIL. Briggs argued that either Asbestos was an agent of JHIL or alternatively, it was an agent of the shareholders and controllers of Asbestos and he was, therefore, entitled to ignore the separate personality of JHIL or Asbestos.[44] Rogers J rejected this saying that 'the effects of incorporation' cannot be displaced by agency principles.[45] His Honour did find merit in the view that where subsidiaries are wholly owned by parent companies, and 'are bound hand and foot to the parent company and must do what the parent company says',[46] the group resembles a partnership.[47] However, the level of control that one company (a parent) exercises over another (a subsidiary) does not of itself justify disregarding the parent company's separate personality.[48] The separate legal entity doctrine is strictly adhered to, even in company groups.

James Hardie's US Business

While the JH group was concerned about its tort liabilities in Australia and their financial costs, their business in the United States (US) had none of these problems. The group's US company manufactured building materials, but unlike Amaba and Amaca in Australia the US company was able to produce *asbestos-free* and affordable building products. The US business was profitable and now the main financial driver of the group's future. This was one of the reasons JHIL later decided to restructure the group to protect its profitable US business and insulate it and the Australian business from the tort liabilities. The US company with its new building product was and remains, the revenue stream for the JH group to pay its asbestos liabilities in Australia.

The legal and practical reality of JHIL as a parent company being made liable for its subsidiaries' tort liabilities was remote. This was not the perception from the US where it was thought these liabilities had the potential to overwhelm the group's profitability, as had happened with US company

---

42 (1997) 44 NSWLR 463.
43 (1989) 16 NSWLR 549.
44 Ibid., 558.
45 Ibid., 575.
46 Ibid., 571.
47 *Harold Holdsworth & Co (Wakefield) Ltd v Caddies* [1955] 1 WLR 352.
48 (1989) 16 NSWLR 549, 577.

Manville. This perception was an obstacle to the group's US stock exchange listing, required to raise capital to exploit JH's intellectual property in its asbestos-free building materials.

JHIL's Decision to Restructure the Group

It was imperative that JHIL act to minimise any risk to the group's profit. Manville's strategies were studied by JHIL to address its tort liability. Manville had undertaken a company reorganisation, or restructure. The board of JHIL also decided to restructure the group, passing a resolution at its meeting in February 2001. It sought to separate itself from its asbestos liability-laden subsidiaries, Amaba and Amaca. The board resolved to create a Medical Research and Compensation Foundation (MRCF). This entailed a sale by JHIL to MRCF, and a transfer of Amaba and Amaca and their assets, to meet current and anticipated asbestos liabilities.[49] Now MRCF would be responsible for the tort liabilities. It would be liable for successful compensation claims made against these former subsidiaries.[50] The new directors of MRCF were assured by JHIL that MRCF was fully funded and had 'sufficient funds to meet anticipated future claims'.[51]

An allocation was made by JHIL to MRCF of A$79 million of its own funds and a further A$214 million, being the value of Amaba and Amaca's net assets.[52] The asbestos liabilities were removed from the JH group's balance sheet as well as 'A$72.4 million in asbestos provisions'.[53]

The restructure also involved a change of jurisdiction for JHIL from Australia to the Netherlands to access lower company taxation. A new parent company, JHI NV, would wholly own JHIL, now a subsidiary, with JHIL's assets being transferred to JHI NV which would hold non-core assets and liabilities.[54] Now JHIL would become ABN 60 Pty Ltd ('ABN 60'), a non-operating shell company: one 'that has ceased operations and has no assets or liabilities'.[55]

49 *Jackson Report,* above n 2, 8 [1.6]

50 Christine Parker and Adrian Evans, *Inside Lawyers' Ethics* (Cambridge University Press, 3rd ed., 2018) 320.

51 *Jackson Report,* above n 2, [22.4] 352.

52 Ibid.

53 Anthony Hughes, 'Hardie Cleans UP its Asbestos Act', *The Sydney Morning Herald,* 17 February 2001, 51 https://www.smh.com.au

54 *Jackson Report,* above n 2, [25.4, 25.5] 421–2.

55 Robert Austin and Ian Ramsay, *Ford, Austin and Ramsay's Principles of Corporations Law* (LexisNexis, 17th ed., 2018) [5.030] 172.

External Lawyers and the Restructure

Allens, JHIL's external lawyers, advised upon the Trowbridge reports which were expected to be a primary source of information for JHIL directors when calculating tort liabilities and the funding needs of MRCF. The adequacy of MRCF's funding was a key element in JHIL's legal disclosure obligations to the Australian Securities Exchange (ASX), and to the Supreme Court which would ultimately need to approve the restructure. These matters are discussed in other Parts, below. Another matter, examined here, was whether JHIL directors' restructure decision complied with their legal duties as fiduciaries to act in JHIL's best interests and for a proper purpose.[56]

Tort Liabilities and the Restructure

Allens was invited by JHIL to attend its February 2001 board meeting to explain the legalities of the restructure. It was not until the morning of the board meeting that Allens discovered there were missing data from the Trowbridge reports.[57] Peter Cameron and David Robb of Allens, spoke to Peter Shafron, JHIL's in-house group counsel, expressing their concern. They were advised that 'Trowbridge said they [Trowbridge] did not require the most recent data and it would not make a difference to their conclusions' as their report concerned longer-term trends.[58] Shafron assured Allens, that MRCF was fully funded.[59] Allens then wrote to JHIL saying it would seek further advice from His Honour Justice Allsop, of the Federal Court.[60] Allens's letter was included in the board papers.

This is an example of a client placing its lawyers in a difficult position professionally. Allens could only give full legal advice when in possession of all relevant facts. Assurances were very belatedly given by JHIL, and only when Allens discovered that there were missing data from the Trowbridge reports. This late notification resulted in Allens having to appear before and advise the board meeting upon expected tort liabilities, when there were information gaps. Commissioner Jackson later noted the 'absence of any substantive discussion in' board papers 'on the actual amount of the

56 *Corporations Act* (Cth) *2001* s 181.

57 Haigh, above n 26, 262–3.

58 *Australian Securities and Investments Commission v Macdonald (No 11)* [2009] NSWSC 287 [328] 105–6 (*'Macdonald case'*).

59 Haigh, above n 26, 262–3.

60 *Jackson Report,* above n 2, [14.27] 189.

asbestos liabilities'.[61] It was alleged elsewhere that the board papers 'openly countenanced the possibility that the Foundation's [MRCF] resources might be insufficient'.[62]

Commissioner Jackson was surprised that the funding issue was not raised earlier, as the concept of a trust (which later became a foundation: MRCF) 'was settled upon in late 2000'[63] and advisors (presumably referring to Allens) knew that the funding had 'to be rigorously checked'.[64] The Commissioner mentioned the lawyer-to-client relationship here when he acknowledged that JHIL's 'management were determined, as far as possible, to deal with the matter in-house … and outside advice' upon its merits, was not welcome.[65] This reflects the position of some major external law firms where much of their power is diminished by the power of their clients.[66] Law firms' ability to give proper advice to clients is inhibited if information is withheld.

JHIL's Directors' Duty to Act in Best Interests

The directors' duty to act in the best interests of the company relates to the common law in 1998–2001 when JHIL's restructure decisions were made. *Darvall v North Sydney Brick & Tile Co. Ltd*[67] held that the duty refers to decisions a reasonable director would make. Further, 'it is not a function of the court to substitute its own opinion for that of the directors' who can determine their own company's best interests.[68] However, directors must have regard to the separate interests 'of the company as a commercial entity' and 'the members'.[69] The duty is owed to the company, not the shareholders, as they 'elect or appoint directors to manage the company for' their benefit.[70] The statutory duty requires directors to act in good faith and in the best interests of the company and for a proper purpose.[71]

---

61 Ibid., [14.13] 181.

62 Haigh, above n 26, 268.

63 *Jackson Report,* above n 2, [29.13] 547.

64 Ibid., [29.14] 547.

65 Ibid.

66 John Flood, 'The Re-Organization and Re-Professionalization of Large Law Firms in the 21st Century: From Patriarchy to Democracy' (2012) 36 *Journal of the Legal Profession* 415, 420.

67 (1987) 16 NSWLR 212.

68 Ibid., 238.

69 Ibid., 239.

70 *Brunninghausen v Glavanics* (1999) 46 NSWLR 538 at 557.

71 *Corporations Act 2001* (Cth) s 181.

According to JHIL's directors, they believed a restructure satisfied a legitimate and lawful purpose: to increase profit and isolate risk by insulating 'the parent's assets from a liability arising' elsewhere in the group.[72] They regarded these reasons as being in JHIL's best interests.[73] It was 'in the best interests of the Company [JHIL] to effect' a separation of it from Amaca and Amaba.[74] It appears Australian law at that time did not permit JHIL directors to consider the interests of both its shareholders and a key stakeholder group, the tort victims.

Best Interests and Stakeholders

Employee stakeholders could exercise their legal rights in the tort of negligence. The restructure decision by JHIL, under company law, gave the same employee stakeholders no recognition. The ethical issues flowing from the restructure were more serious for employee stakeholders who were ill and would receive inadequate compensation due to funding shortfalls. Shareholders were only indirectly affected. This made it even more important for lawyers to give JHIL ethical advice regarding tort stakeholders.

In *Darvall v North Sydney Brick & Tile Co. Ltd*[75] Hodgson J held best interests 'should not be narrow' and it was proper to also regard the interests of stakeholders other than member shareholders, such as company creditors.[76] Tort victims whose claims are proven and have a liquidated judgement, are company creditors. Those asbestos claimants whose claims were yet to be made may not fall within the category of interests to be considered in discharging the best interests' duty. Therefore, these claimants were insufficiently considered in the funding of MRCF. They could not be considered when directors did not know the quantum of successful future tort claims, but it was possible to estimate future claims from actuarial reports.

There was no clear commercial benefit for JHIL in reserving compensation for the future tort victim stakeholders, who did not yet have a liquidated claim. The law, therefore, was enabling an unethical decision by JHIL directors to underfund the MRCF and limit their responsibility. This and limited liability law as well as the separate legal entity principle served to further diminish JHIL's responsibility. This intersection of the law and

---

72 Austin and Ramsay, above n 56, [4.270] 160.

73 Paul Redmond, 'Directors' Duties and Corporate Social Responsiveness' (2012) 35(1) *University of New South Wales Law Journal* 317, 319.

74 *Jackson Report,* above n 2, [14.50] 199–200.

75 (1987) 16 NSWLR 212.

76 Ibid., 239.

ethics is addressed in a subsequent funding solution below, approved by Commissioner Jackson.

Bell Group Ltd (in liq.) v Westpac Banking Corporation (No. 9)[77] provides insight into the future direction of the common law. Owen J held that directors' duty to act in best interests is not entirely subjective and that 'the court can look objectively at the surrounding circumstances ... in relation to exercise by the directors of their power'.[78] Further, 'the court may intervene if the [directors' decision] is such that no reasonable board of directors could think the decision to be in the best interests of the company'.[79]

There needs to be a clear basis on which directors can act simultaneously both legally and ethically and this is precisely where the new moral TLE model could play an important role. In addition, the non-employee stakeholders (those exposed to the hazards of asbestos products[80] when engaged in building work and renovations) continue to suffer from JH group's decision to use asbestos in building products. These people are outside the protection of workplace laws that applied to Amaba and Amaca employees.

The Restructure and Best Interests

Allen's approval of the restructure was ethically fraught. Asbestos tort victims employed by JH companies could now only rely upon MRCF for compensation. As indicated above, JHIL's allocation to MRCF involved A$79 million of its own funds, plus a further A$214 million, being the value of Amaba and Amaca's net assets.[81] No further funds could be added by JHIL because a consequence of the restructure was that JHIL's remaining assets were transferred to a new parent company: JHI NV[82] and JHIL was now a shell company, ABN 60.[83]

If JHIL could quarantine in MRCF any liability it or its subsidiaries might have, it was then difficult to justify to JHIL shareholders that it was in JHIL's best interests to transfer additional company assets for future tort creditors, as they were now MRCF's responsibility.[84] Allens advised the JHIL board in the February meeting that JHIL could *not* now legally pro-

---

77 [2008] WASC 239.
78 Ibid., [4619].
79 Ibid.
80 Nick Toscano, 'Renovators Drive New Wave of James Hardie Asbestos Claims', *The Sydney Morning Herald,* 22 May 2018 https://www.smh.com.au
81 Parker and Evans, above n 50, 320.
82 *Jackson Report,* above n 2, [1.6] 8.
83 Parker and Evans, above n 50, 322.
84 *Jackson Report,* above n 2, [30.22] 557.

vide MRCF with additional funds unless it had an honest belief it was in JHIL's best interests.[85] Reputation enhancement, as a result of providing additional funds to MRCF, might have been considered in the group's best interests. However, its main business was in the US with only 15 per cent 'of its revenue derived in Australia', and the small reputation boost it could receive from extra funds could not be justified under best interests.[86]

Commissioner Jackson later noted that solicitors (from various firms) acting for JHIL, Amaca, Amaba, and MRCF, seemed almost entirely focussed upon the law of directors' duties.[87] This was the main concern of JHIL's instructions to their lawyers. The Commissioner noted the concentration upon directors' duties whilst 'the subjects to which the duties relate' and 'the merits of the underlying transactions' were ignored.[88] This is a statement about ethics and demonstrates the effect of lawyers' positivist TLE which directs lawyers not to consider ethical issues.

The merits of key underlying transactions referred to by Commissioner Jackson were JHIL's restructure and funding provisions for MRCF. These were not just decisions related to a duty at law, here best interests, they also concerned ethics in relation to tort victims and their compensation. Lawyers, by the nature of their work, ought not to have the limited role given to them by a positivist TLE only to interpret the law. The ethical issues they encounter require more than this. Lawyers could have a broader and more fulfilling professional role under a moral TLE that permits them to examine ethical issues identified in client instructions. Then lawyers could consider the merits of those underlying transactions. Addressing ethical issues is in the best interests of companies, commercially and for their business reputation. It is also said that good ethics is good business.[89]

The legal question is whether JHIL's directors knew at the time of the restructure that MRCF's funding was inadequate. If they did know, then the funding issue made the restructure at least unethical and possibly a breach of best interests' duty. There was confusion by both parties concerning the Trowbridge reports regarding asbestos claims. Managing director Macdonald, and legal counsel Shafron, knew there were data missing from these reports in 2000 (April–December),[90] yet JHIL had declined to provide

---

85 Ibid., [14.45] 196.
86 Redmond, above n 74, 328.
87 *Jackson Report,* above n 2, [29.16] 548.
88 Ibid.
89 Robert Solomon, 'It's Good Business' in William Shaw, Vincent Barry, and George Sansbury (eds) *Moral Issues in Business* (Cengage Learning, 2009) 37.
90 *Jackson Report,* above n 2, [24.71] 416.

data when requested by Trowbridge, and Shafron, stated Trowbridge had said they did not need it.[91]

JHIL's ASX Disclosure Obligation

The February 2001 board meeting of JHIL approved both the group's restructure and JHIL's subsequent announcement to the ASX. A company restructure is price-sensitive information as it is likely to 'have a material effect on the price or value' of that company's securities.[92] Public listed companies, such as JHIL, have legal obligations under the continuous disclosure regime to immediately and accurately inform the market of such information.[93]

ASX Announcement

A key element of JHIL's ASX announcement and subsequent media release regarding MRCF's establishment was unequivocal statements that MRCF's funds were adequate to meet future claims. This was a representation by JHIL to the ASX, JHIL shareholders, tort victims, the market generally, and the public. It said in part:

> A *fully funded* Foundation [MRCF] … provides *certainty* … *'James Hardie is satisfied* that the Foundation has *sufficient funds* to meet anticipated future claims' [Macdonald, MD] … James Hardie sought expert advice from [actuaries] … When all future claims have been concluded, *surplus funds* will be used to support further scientific and medical research of lung diseases.[94]

Commissioner Jackson stated 'the ordinary reader' would deduce from the media release that JHIL was saying MRCF funds would 'meet all legitimate compensation claims anticipated from people injured by asbestos products that were manufactured in the past'.[95] They would also believe JHIL had sought expert advice from actuaries and accountants regarding MRCF's funding;[96] and that the Foundation was fully funded, thereby providing

---

91 Ibid., [24.4] 391.
92 *Corporations Act 2001* (Cth) s 674(2).
93 Ibid., s 674(1); ASX Listing Rules, r 3.1 https://www.asx.com.au
94 *Jackson Report,* above n 2, [22.4] 352 (emphasis added).
95 Ibid., [22.8] 354.
96 Ibid., [22.11] 355.

'certainty for both claimants and shareholders'.[97] Commissioner Jackson opined that the announcement 'seems a pure public relations construct, bereft of substantial truth',[98] and further, that Macdonald (JHIL managing director and CEO) knew it was false.[99]

The ASX announcement had multiple legal consequences for JHIL. The corporate regulator, the Australian Securities and Investments Commission (ASIC) took legal action in *Australian Securities and Investments Commission v Macdonald*[100] (*Macdonald case*) against all JHIL directors, including Peter Macdonald, Phillip Morley (chief financial officer), and Peter Shafron (group counsel and company secretary) for breaches of their duty of care and diligence. The Court held the case against all directors had been made out. The ASX announcement contained false or misleading statements and directors had taken insufficient steps to ensure its accuracy (such as including actuarial or other qualifications on the extent of the claims that MRCF would fund).[101] In addition, the case against Macdonald had been made out as he had breached this duty 'in approving for release the Final ASX Announcement'.[102] The non-executive directors appealed the decision: *Morley v Australian Securities and Investments Commission*, and this was upheld.[103] A successful appeal was made by ASIC to the High Court in *Australian Securities and Investments Commission v Hellicar*[104] to reinstate the decision at first instance: that all directors had indeed breached their statutory duty of care.

Legal action was also taken by ASIC against JHIL for its contraventions of market disclosure law[105] and misleading and deceptive market misconduct.[106] In addition, making false or misleading statements to the market that are likely to induce persons to sell or purchase securities.[107] The Court in the *Macdonald case* held the breaches of these laws had been made out.[108] An appeal by the new parent company that replaced JHIL, was later

---

97 Ibid., [22.12] 356.
98 Ibid., [22.22] 358.
99 Ibid., [22.48] 367, [22.56] 370.
100 [2009] NSWSC 287.
101 Ibid., [1269]–[1270] 335.
102 Ibid., [1281] 337.
103 [2010] NSWCA 331.
104 [2012] HCA 17.
105 *Corporations Act, 2001* (Cth) s674(1).
106 Ibid., s 995(2) [now s 1041H].
107 Ibid., s 999 [now s 1041E]: a criminal offence.
108 [2009] NSWSC 287 at [1282] 338 re
        s 995(2) [s 1041H]; at [1283] 338 re ss 674, 999 [s 1041E], *Corporations Act, 2001* (Cth).

dismissed: *James Hardie Industries NV v Australian Securities Investments Commission.*[109]

It was also alleged by ASIC in the *Macdonald case* that Macdonald was in breach of his best interests' duty in relation to JHIL's ASX announcement and in JHIL's statements at press conferences in Australia and in the UK.[110] Although Macdonald presided over JHIL, and its breaches of the *Corporations Act:* ss 674(1), 995(2), and 999 had been proven, the Court held that Macdonald had not contravened his best interests' duty.[111] The Court followed the reasoning in *Marchesi v Barnes* where Gowans J held best interests required subjective dishonesty, 'a consciousness that what is being done is not in the interests of the company'.[112] Later, as noted above, Owens J in *Bell Group Ltd (in liq.) v Westpac Banking Corporation,* held that courts will intervene 'if the decision is such that no reasonable board of directors could think the decision to be in the interests of the company'.[113]

JHIL's In-House Lawyer

The position of Shafron is instructive to appreciate the role of senior in-house lawyers. Shafron was also company secretary. It was alleged by ASIC in the *Macdonald case* that Shafron as group counsel had breached his duty of care as he had 'failed to advise the board that' the draft ASX announcement was 'too emphatic' concerning the ability of MRCF 'to meet all legitimate present and future' tort claims.[114] The Court held that as both group counsel and company secretary, Shafron had participated in decisions affecting JHIL.[115] This made him a company 'officer'[116] of JHIL and subject to the duties of officers[117] as well as his duty to JHIL as a senior lawyer. These positions gave Shafron a high degree of responsibility to protect JHIL from legal risks associated with the ASX announcement[118] such as the risk of JHIL engaging in prohibited market conduct by making false or misleading statements.[119] The Court held that Shafron 'failed to discharge his

---

109 [2010] NSWCA 332.
110 [2009] NSWSC 287 at [26] 13; [44] 20.
111 Ibid., [1286] 338; [1296] 340; [1308] 342.
112 [1970] VR 434 at 438.
113 [2008] WASC 239 at [4619]
114 [2009] NSWSC 287 at [1271] 335.
115 Ibid., [393] 122.
116 *Corporations Act 2001* (Cth) s 9(b)(i).
117 [2009] NSWSC 287 at [386] 120–1.
118 Ibid., [398] 124.
119 Ibid., [402] 124.

duties to JHIL with the degree of care and diligence that a reasonable person would exercise' as an officer who was company secretary, and as group counsel.[120] Shafron's appeal was partially successful: *Morley v Australian Securities and Investments Commission,*[121] a case that also heard appeals from directors. Shafron again appealed, this time to the High Court, *Shafron v Australian Securities and Investments Commission*[122] on the grounds that:

> if he was an officer only because he was a company secretary, his obligations under s 180(1) were limited to the exercise of powers and discharge of duties as secretary, without regard to any powers of duties as general counsel.[123]

Shafron had separated his roles. He argued his participation in board decisions was part of 'his responsibilities as company secretary [and these] did not extend to tendering that advice' upon the legalities of the ASX announcement.[124] Therefore, failing to give this advice to the board was not a breach of duty of care for a company secretary, whose role was administrative. The Court disagreed and held his responsibilities were more than administrative and 'extended to the provision of necessary advice'.[125]

We are now able to appreciate the nuances of the corporate lawyer-to-client relationship when the client, JHIL, was prepared to issue an announcement to the ASX that the managing director knew was false[126] and 'ought reasonably to have known ... was false in material particulars, and materially misleading'.[127] Shafron, as company secretary and group counsel, was at least negligent in not preventing this statement to the ASX.[128]

JHIL's External Lawyers and ASX Disclosure

Actuarial reports intended to inform the board and management of JHIL's position in relation to MRCF's funds, were incomplete, with data missing, but Allens discovered this on the day of JHIL's board meeting.[129] The

---

120   Ibid., [406] 125.
121   [2010]) NSWCA 331.
122   [2012] HCA 18.
123   Ibid., [8] 18.
124   Ibid.
125   Ibid., [15].
126   *Jackson Report,* above n 2, [22.48] 367.
127   Ibid., [22.56] 370.
128   [2012] HCA at [15] 18.
129   Haigh, above n 26, 262.

Macdonald case revealed Shafron only then informed Allens that this data would make no difference to the conclusion that there were sufficient funds, as Trowbridge's report concerned longer-term trends.[130] It appears that Allens may have been misled by its client who was prepared to hide important facts from Allens that were crucial to MRCF funding.

Yet, with all of these factors in play, Gzell J in the *Macdonald case* found Allens prepared draft minutes of the JHIL board meeting some time *before* the February board meeting was held and these included an anticipated resolution to approve a draft ASX announcement.[131] The accuracy of the ASX announcement was examined and Gzell J asked why neither Cameron nor Robb, from Allens, reacted 'to the unequivocal and unqualified statements when they read their copies of the draft ASX announcement at the 15 February meeting'.[132] Gzell J's answer was that: 'Mr Cameron accepted the term "fully funded" as appropriate' and that earlier on the day of the meeting, they had been appraised of a new development that they had yet to analyse.[133] This was that the Trowbridge report had omitted several months of the most recent data on tort claims.[134] This could raise doubts about the ASX announcement and any assertion that the tort claims were able to be fully funded.

Allens relied upon Shafron's assurances as a senior lawyer and an insider at JHIL, that the information he chose to give was reliable and complete. It was not, but Allens nevertheless felt compelled to approve the legality of the announcement even though they were yet to receive further advice they had sought from a Federal Court Judge.[135] The fact that under these circumstances Allens approved the ASX announcement could indicate the pressure they were under from the client as well as the client-directed role that lawyers are encouraged to accept under a positivist TLE model. This model undermines lawyers' professional independence. Importantly, this served neither the lawyers nor their clients.

Court Approval of JHIL's Restructure

A company restructure occurs under the legal process of a scheme of arrangement (Scheme).[136] This requires judicial approval by the Supreme

---

130   [2009] NSWSC 287 [328] 105–6.
131   Ibid., [1192] 320.
132   Ibid., [327] 105.
133   Ibid.
134   Ibid., [328] 105–6.
135   *Jackson Report,* above n 2, [14.27] 189.
136   *Corporations Act, 2001* (Cth) ss 411, 412(1)(a).

Court. A court hearing commenced in August 2001 before Santow J. The Court had to be satisfied that JHIL's Scheme would protect the rights of stakeholders, here, JHIL shareholders and asbestos tort claimants.[137]

JHIL's Disclosure Duties to the Court

The statutory duties under a Scheme[138] complement the disclosure duties to the Court of 'both JHIL and its lawyers'.[139] In its application to the Court, JHIL proposed that its shareholders would exchange their shares for shares in the new parent company, James Hardie Industries NV (JHI NV), and JHI NV would subscribe 'to partly paid shares in JHIL'[140] This was conditional upon JHIL being able to call upon 'JHI NV to pay any or all of the remainder of the issue price of these shares at any time in the future'.[141] The purpose here was to give JHIL 'access to cash if required in the future to meet any liabilities'.[142] It was expected there would be 100,000 partly paid shares subject to this call, worth an estimated A$1.9 billion.[143]

Santow J, indicated at the Scheme's first hearing day in August 2001, that he was aware that the partly paid shares were intended to protect JHIL's tort victims.[144] The *Macdonald case* found that if MRCF, which had primary responsibility to pay successful compensation claims against Amaba and Amaca, experienced a funding shortfall, Allens advised that JHIL might be held liable.[145] If so, JHIL would then make a call on the new parent company, JHI NV. Shareholders of JHIL would be sent an explanatory statement[146] with a notice of a meeting at which they would vote upon and consent to the Scheme.[147] This statement had to include sufficient relevant information for consent to be given in good faith and the Scheme had to be 'sufficiently fair and reasonable that an intelligent and honest shareholder or creditor … might approve it'.[148] The JHIL shareholders consented to the Scheme and it was later approved by the Court on 11 October 2001.[149]

---

137 *Jackson Report,* above n 2, [25.26] 433.
138 *Corporations Act, 2001* (Cth) ss 411(1), 411(4)(b).
139 *Jackson Report,* above n 2, [25.35] 436.
140 Ibid., [25.5] 423.
141 Ibid., [25.17] 429.
142 Ibid., [25.16] 429.
143 Ibid., [25.1–25.18] 429.
144 Ibid., [25.37] 436.
145 [2009] NSWSC 287 [908] 251.
146 *Corporations Act, 2001* (Cth) ss 411, 412(1)(a).
147 Ibid., s 411.
148 Austin and Ramsay, above n 56, [24.160] 1720.
149 *Jackson Report,* above n 2, [25.26] 433.

Cancellation of the Partly Paid Shares

Within 18 months of the Scheme's approval, the partly paid shares were cancelled. The possibility of cancellation was not disclosed to the Court,[150] JHIL's shareholders, or Allens. The effect of the cancellation was to deny JHIL access to A$1.9 billion[151] and to remove this source of funds for tort claimants.

Later in the *Macdonald case*, ASIC alleged Macdonald was negligent in relation to draft correspondence sent to Justice Santow's associate. This stated that 'JHIL would have, through existing reserves and access to funding in the form of partly paid shares, the means to meet [its future] liabilities', but the Court found ASIC failed to prove this allegation.[152]

Morley, JHIL's chief financial officer, indicated as early as March 2001 that it was likely that upon completion of the restructure, 'the partly paid shares would be regarded as "an unnecessary capital lifeline" and [were] likely to be cancelled'.[153] Commissioner Jackson interpreted an email from in-house counsel, Shafron, as suggesting the purpose of the partly paid shares was 'a device to avoid an examination by the court of the extent of the liabilities of JHIL'.[154] The 'separation of JHIL ... from the group had *never ceased to be an objective ... and this included 'cancellation of the partly paid shares'*.[155]

In 2006 JHI NV, the group's new parent company replacing JHIL, revealed JHIL's thinking at the time of the cancellation in 2003. In an explanatory memorandum to shareholders in another matter[156] it said that the then JHIL had reviewed the assets and current and future liabilities of Amaba and Amaca (now transferred to MRCF) under the 2001 Deed of Covenant and Indemnity (under the Scheme).[157] This review showed a net liability of A$76 million and total assets of A$94.5 million and as this was sufficient to meet present and future liabilities, the partly paid shares were no longer needed[158] and could be cancelled.

The defence JHIL used for its disclosure failures was twofold. First, it stated that it did not intend to cancel the partly paid shares. In the alternative, it stated that in capital reductions (as the Scheme was classified) the

---

150 Ibid., [25.29] 434.
151 Ibid., [26.67] 512.
152 [2009] NSWSC 287: [1301] 341 and [1302] 341.
153 *Jackson Report,* above n 2, [25.67] 450.
154 Ibid., [25.69] 450.
155 Ibid., [25.71] 451 (emphasis added).
156 James Hardie Industries NV, *Explanatory Memorandum,* 12 December 2006 https://ir
     .jameshardie.com.au/public/download.jsp?id=2054
157 Ibid., 18.
158 Ibid.

Court is presumed to be aware of the possibility of share cancellation.[159] It is legally permissible to buy back shares under a capital reduction[160] and to cancel them.[161] Shafron emailed Morley and Macdonald regarding a letter to MRCF, that referred to cancellation of the shares, saying that this was 'an arrangement which has been in contemplation since the beginning'.[162] The Commissioner found the 'operating assumption' on which both management and the board were proceeding was that the shares would be cancelled 'within a year or so of the restructure'.[163] Assurances were given by JHIL to the Court and Allens regarding these shares yet those statements contradicted JHIL's intentions.

Between May and September 2001 the managing directors of MRCF and JHIL were meeting regularly to discuss MRCF's funding concerns.[164] Directors of MRCF communicated with JHIL's Macdonald,[165] seeking more funds. Contemporaneously (in August 2001), JHIL was appearing in the Supreme Court arguing that there were enough funds for tort claimants. Commissioner Jackson noted that MRCF's communications with JHIL were not disclosed to Santow J,[166] yet they would have revealed MRCF's funding concerns. The Commissioner found that JHIL had breached its duty of disclosure by failing to disclose this.[167]

JHIL's External Lawyers and Duties to the Court

The partly paid shares and related non-disclosures were important issues for Allens. It needed full disclosure from JHIL to prepare its case. Lawyers have their own disclosure duty to the Court. Santow J asked Allens to explain the effect of the Scheme on the 'asbestos claims'.[168] The *Macdonald case* revealed that in August 2001, Allens wrote to Shafron and to Santow J's associate:

> [i]t cannot be said that JHIL will never be held liable. JHIL will have, through existing reserves and access to funding in the form of the partly

159 *Jackson Report,* n 2, [25.59] 444.
160 *Corporations Act 2001* (Cth) ss 257B–257H.
161 Ibid., s 258E.
162 *Jackson Report,* n 2, [25.79] 453.
163 Ibid., [25.80] 453.
164 Ibid., [25.39] 437–8.
165 Ibid., [20.74] 323.
166 Ibid., [25.29] 434.
167 Ibid., [25.91] 456.
168 Ibid., [25.34] 436.

paid shares, the means to meet liabilities which will or may arise in the future whether in relation to asbestos related claims or other obligations to other persons.[169]

If Allens was perceived as failing to disclose any knowledge it may have had of either JHIL's intention to cancel the partly paid shares or the true funding position of MRCF, this could indicate it was misleading the Court. This was relevant to the Scheme's approval as Santow J regarded the protection of asbestos tort victims as integral to this approval. Lawyers' disclosure duty is part of their general law duties to the court and the administration of justice.[170]

Allens stated in submissions to the Court that it 'had no reason to believe JHIL intended to cancel the shares'.[171] Allens referred to written material involving JHIL directors and officers: memoranda, emails, minutes of JHIL board meetings, as well as Allens's own file notes.[172] Allens argued these showed no intention by JHIL to cancel the partly paid shares.[173] Commissioner Jackson responded that Allens's 'submissions *inappropriately* confine the area of inquiry to the period from March 2001' reflecting JHIL board's view that 'post-restructure plans for JHIL … did not need to be disclosed'.[174] However, this was no 'basis for [Allens] concluding that they [JHIL] had no such plans'.[175] Allens argued, as did JHIL: 'that all share capital is cancellable' under the *Corporations Act* and the Court could be assumed to be aware of this.[176]

Commissioner Jackson said it was necessary to examine disclosure in a factual context and that JHIL had stated explicitly that 'the partly paid shares would be available in the future' and 'the judge made it clear that the efficacy of that "capital lifeline" was a matter of concern'.[177] Under these circumstances JHIL's plans should have been disclosed as JHIL board, senior management, and Allens, were all 'familiar with JHIL's internal strategic planning over the 1998–2001 period'.[178] They knew 'the true purpose

---

169 [2009] NSWSC 287 [908] 251.
170 GE Dal Pont, *Lawyers' Professional Responsibility* (Thomson Reuters, 7th ed., 2021) [17.05] 570.
171 *Jackson Report,* above n 2, [25.59] 444.
172 Ibid., [25.81] 453–4.
173 Ibid.
174 Ibid., [25.82] 455, emphasis added.
175 Ibid.
176 Ibid., [25.83] 455.
177 Ibid., [25.86] 455.
178 Ibid., [25.87] 456.

of the partly paid shares [that is] (stakeholder management), [and] would have formed the view that their cancellation was almost inevitable'.[179] Professionally, Allens ought to have asserted its independence by making further inquiries to ensure it and JHIL met their disclosure duties at law.

The Commissioner's conclusions were damning. Allens and JHIL had both breached their legal duties 'of disclosure in the proceedings before Santow J' concerning the likely cancellation of the partly paid shares, although this breach was not deliberate'.[180] The Commissioner found that Allens had also breached 'its duty of care to JHIL', but 'it is not clear that any such breach caused JHIL loss'.[181]

The JH group's new parent company, JHI NV, had made some very serious allegations in its Initial Submissions to the Inquiry regarding JHIL *or*, in the alternative, Allens.[182] It said that they had: engaged in misleading and deceptive conduct under the then *Trade Practices Act*;[183] 'and attempted to pervert the cause of justice, and that the orders of Santow J [to approve the Scheme] … [had been] procured by fraud'.[184] If these allegations had been proven, it would have been disastrous for Allens and almost impossible for this leading law firm to maintain its credibility. Fortunately, these initial submissions were 'disavowed in final, oral submissions' and Commissioner Jackson accepted this although he stated that 'in fact it was in mind as arguable at the time of the cancellation' of the shares.[185]

MRCF Funding Shortfall

Asbestos claims and related costs involving Amaca's former employees for the years ending 31 March 2000 and 31 March 2001 were compared by MRCF which found that the 2001 costs were significantly higher than predictions.[186] Claims deriving from Amaca were A$18.3 million for the 12 months to 31 March 2000, and an expected A$37.6 million for the 15 months to 30 June 2001.[187] By April 2001, the increasing volume of tort

---

179 Ibid.

180 Ibid., [25.91] 456.

181 Ibid.

182 JHI NV Initial Submissions, [16.1.3] cited in the *Jackson Report* [25.91] 457, footnote 103.

183 *Trade Practices Act 1974* (Cth) s 52; [now *Competition and Consumer Act 2010* (Cth) Australian Consumer Law, s 18, sch 2].

184 *Jackson Report,* above n 2, [25.91] 457.

185 Ibid., (emphasis added).

186 Ibid., [20.72] 323.

187 Ibid., [26.1] 459.

claims indicated that the financial resources of MRCF were being rapidly diminished and the expected lifespan of its funds to meet claims emanating from Amaca had halved from 20 to 10 years.[188] At this point it was reasonable to presume some future claims would be unmet. By May 2001 the directors of MRCF were already meeting regularly with JHIL's management about the adequacy of the liability provisions.[189]

By July 2002, MRCF was using updated Trowbridge reports with claim projections of A$810 million, resulting in a depletion to zero of MRCF funds within five years.[190] That the funding issue was urgent is shown in a February 2003 letter to JHIL's Macdonald, now managing director of JHI NV, from MRCF's managing director, Sir Llew Edwards:

> ... contrary to the indications given to ourselves, the government and to the community in public statements, our assets are expected to last only some four to five years, with some *80% of future victims being unlikely to have their claims considered let alone met.*[191]

The partly paid shares were cancelled on 15 March 2003. When we consider the above letter sent the month before, it seems there was no economic (or ethical) reason to cancel these shares as further funds were needed.

JHIL's External Lawyers and MRCF

Macdonald's response throughout these travails was to reiterate Allens's legal advice to JHIL's board at its February 2001 meeting.[192] This was that JHIL could not legally provide MRCF with additional funds unless it had an honest belief this was in JHIL's best interests.[193] This restricted legal interpretation of JHIL's best interests was current at this time. This is why 'the JH group was adamant no further substantial funds would be made available' to MRCF[194] and the group had no other responsibility under the best interests' duty as it had now quarantined in MRCF, 'liabilities in the former subsidiaries'.[195] The legal position meant the law provided the JH group with a shield from further funding of MRCF. It appears ethical argu-

188 Ibid., [20.73] 323.
189 Ibid., [25.39], 437–8.
190 Ibid., [26.75] 483.
191 *Jackson Report,* above n 2, [27.22] 496, emphasis added.
192 Haigh, above n 26, 328.
193 *Jackson Report,* above n 2, [14.45] 196.
194 Ibid., [1.22], 12.
195 Redmond, above n 74, 318.

ments were not considered. Nor could they be under a positivist TLE as it is not the lawyers' role to identify ethical matters. Therefore, it was an option for JHIL directors in acting in the best interests of JHIL, to effectively deny funds to future claimants.

Allens advised JHIL that MRCF could not claim from JHIL (now a shell company) and Commissioner Jackson agreed.[196] Again, this was the legal position. MRCF then asked JHI NV, the new parent company, for funds and it said it had no legal liability to fund MRCF.[197] As a newly incorporated holding company, JHI NV had had no legal relationship with the former operating subsidiaries, Amaba and Amaca. Lawyers for JHIL and MRCF would have been aware that tort victims could only claim from MRCF. This was the significance of the need for MRCF to be properly funded.

Lawyers for MRCF knew that many claims were yet to be made and the expected liabilities would remain uncertain. Funding *future* tort claimants was, by its nature, a forecast. The number and quantum of claims were impossible to estimate and MRCF's funding shortfalls could only be speculative. Tort law determines the right of tort victims to claim, but company law applies where tortfeasors are companies. Company law neither recognises nor requires reserves for 'unascertained, future creditors, such as future claimants'.[198]

The directors of MRCF took legal action to obtain more funds: *Edwards v Attorney General (NSW)*.[199] The Court held future tort creditors 'do not have a completed cause of action until damage is suffered and that usually involves manifestations of the disease'.[200] It is only then, and following a court decision in their favour, that victims become tort creditors. Until that time, no future claims on MRCF can crystallise and, therefore, cannot be met.[201] This made it impossible to lodge a formal claim against MRCF on behalf of future creditors.

However, actuarial projections and the quantum of damages for past claims assist in forecasting funding requirements. Estimates can be made, and they were, as a prelude to a new funding arrangement demanded by Commissioner Jackson and lawyers for the tort victims. There was public outrage at this time, directed at the JH group when it became clear that it was quarantining liability in MRCF whose funds were finite and could soon be exhausted.

---

196 Parker and Evans, above n 50, 321.
197 Ibid., 323.
198 *Jackson Report,* above n 2, [30.3] 551.
199 [2004] NSWCA 272.
200 Ibid., [58].
201 Ibid., [60].

James Hardie's New Funding Arrangement

A key outcome of the *Jackson Inquiry* was an agreement between the James Hardie parent company, JHIL (later JHI NV) and the NSW Government to provide for long term funding to meet the group's asbestos liabilities.[202] All parties before the Commission agreed MRCF's funding arrangements 'to manage its liabilities are inadequate'.[203] Commissioner Jackson explained that Schemes under the *Corporations Act* did not recognise 'the position of persons in the category of unascertained, future creditors'[204] such as future tort claimants upon MRCF. They would principally rely upon Amaba's and Amaca's assets having been transferred to MRCF. However, in September 2004, the date of the Commission's report, it was anticipated that the funds derived from these two companies would be depleted by 2007,[205] thereby denying compensation for future victims. By 30 September 2006, actuaries estimated that the total liability of these former companies would exceed A$1.5 billion.[206]

The proposed funding arrangement by James Hardie's parent company to assist future claimants occurred in the context of ethical breaches and a narrow interpretation of the best interest duty in company law. However, JHIL could only consider its shareholder members; and what JHIL saw as a financial matter for the group. Significantly, Commissioner Jackson addressed ethical and financial issues when he referred to the morality of the funding shortfall, saying:

> [There] is an economic consideration that may reinforce a *moral judg-ment* that companies in the position of JHI NV should not deny assis-tance to the victims of Amaca and Amaba.[207]

The former parent company, JHIL, had received substantial benefits from these companies. In 2004 values (the date of the *Jackson Report)*, dividends paid by Amaca to JHIL from 1969–1997 were A$2.4 billion, before tax.[208] These profits were retained by new parent company, JHI NV, and were 'large enough to satisfy most, perhaps all', tort claims.[209]

---

202 JHI NV, above n 158, 2 [1.2].
203 *Jackson Report,* above n 2, [30.3] 551.
204 Ibid.
205 Ibid., [30.6] 553.
206 JHI NV, above n 158, [8.3.3] 30.
207 *Jackson Report,* above n 2, [30.14] 555 (emphasis in original).
208 Ibid.
209 Ibid., (emphasis added).

There were several legal avenues for former employees of Amaba and Amaca to make tort claims upon MRCF against their former employers. These included the Dust Diseases Board and Tribunal, claims under workers' compensation legislation, and common law tort claims. When the *Jackson Report* was complete the NSW Government threatened to pass legislation to seize the assets of the JH companies to satisfy judgements in favour of the tort victims. This threat brought JHI NV to the table to 'hammer out' the final settlement which, still to this day, pays those claimants suffering from asbestos-related disease.

A Final Funding Agreement was negotiated by JHI NV, its wholly-owned Performing Subsidiary (James Hardie 117 Pty Ltd), the Asbestos Injuries Compensation Fund Ltd (the trustee), and the NSW Government.[210] The Performing Subsidiary would provide funds to the trustee: initially A$184.3 million, and then at 35 per cent of JH's 'free cash' flow of the preceding financial year.[211] A guarantee was given by JH 'to the Trustee and the NSW Government of the payment obligations of the Performing Subsidiary'.[212] The details of the Final Funding Agreement were given by JHI NV to its shareholders in its Explanatory Memorandum[213] of 12 December 2006, which shareholders approved.

The liabilities of James Hardie group increased in 2018 by 12 per cent to A$195 million reflecting 700 reported cases of the asbestos-related disease mesothelioma, each year in Australia.[214] More than half of these cases concerned home renovators exposed to asbestos fibres from the group's products.[215] The community was a significant stakeholder in the JH case. It was ignorant of the health hazards of asbestos as no warnings were placed on the company's fibro products until 1978.[216] These products were widely used throughout Australia in homes and buildings (exterior and interior walls, roofing, eaves, pipes, and other uses) as 'insulation materials (loose fill, spray on, pipe wrappings) and in brake linings.'[217]

Conclusion

The case study demonstrates that corporate clients such as JHIL may present both legal and ethical dilemmas for lawyers. Company law made it

---

210 JHI NV, above n 158, [1.2] 2–3.

211 Ibid., [1.2] 3.

212 Ibid.

213 Ibid.

214 Toscano, above n 81.

215 Ibid.

216 ACTU *James Hardie Asbestos Victims Compensation Background Facts,* 8 February 2007, p 3 ww.actu.org.au

217 *Jackson Report,* above n 2, [2.1], 17.

possible for clients to act unethically in relation to the provision of funds to compensate tort victims. Appreciating the nature of these problems enables lawyers to better understand corporate clients, the commercial context of their matters, and how ethical issues arise. In legal practice ethical issues are closely linked to professional legal obligations. Consequently, lawyers are professionally vulnerable if clients' decisions made in the progress of legal matters are unethical. The case study shows that positivist TLE did not assist lawyers legally or professionally.

Public anger was directed at JHIL's lawyers as it appeared to the public that legal advice had sanctioned JHIL's unethical conduct. This detracts from the public's ideal of the legal profession and their legal ethics. Allens's advice was used by JHIL as a shield from public criticism in two areas. In relation to the law, JHIL argued that Allens had advised it could not legally give additional funding to MRCF once the Scheme had been approved as this would constitute a breach of JHIL directors' duty to act in JHIL's best interests.[218] In relation to ethics, JHIL could correctly argue that Allens gave it no ethical advice. If lawyers could give both legal and ethical advice this would better serve clients, lawyers, and the public.

Chapter 4 examines a positivist TLE in more detail and applies this model to the ethical issues identified in the JH case. This enables us to appreciate the effectiveness of a positivist TLE. It is important to note that this model of TLE was never intended to address today's complex business strategies and related ethical concerns. While positivist TLE may suit some clients due to its client-centred focus, it creates professional and ethical problems for lawyers in all areas of legal practice.

218 Ibid., [14.45] 196.

4 Theoretical Legal Ethics

Positivist v Moral Principles

Empirical research has shown that theoretical legal ethics (TLE) is influential in legal practice.[1] Accordingly, Chapter 4 analyses the elements of positivist TLE and an alternative: a moral concept of TLE. Contributions to the debate by prominent writers across three jurisdictions – Australia, US, and UK – are analysed.

Positivists separate law and ethics arguing that this enhances the validity of law, and that morality is not a requirement of legality.[2] Moral theorists maintain that morality ought to be at the forefront of lawyers' TLE[3] because this supports their role as professionals where a high standard of integrity is expected. Positivists' have a client-centred view with clients' interests being paramount.[4] These interests sometimes contradict lawyers' professional duties whereby complying with clients' demands may challenge lawyers' legal obligation to fulfil their professional duties.

Moral theorists are mindful that TLE should support integrity in lawyers' role as professionals as they are 'subject to the demands of the moral point of view'.[5] Chapter 4 applies positivist TLE to key decisions of the lawyers in the James Hardie (JH) case to demonstrate the influence of TLE upon both lawyers' advice to clients and the consequent decisions of clients.

---

1 Richard Moorhead and Victoria Hinchly, 'Professional Minimalism? The Ethical Consciousness of Commercial Lawyers' (2015) 42(3) *Journal of Law and Society* 387; Christine Parker and Adrian Evans, *Inside Lawyers' Ethics* (Cambridge University Press, 3rd ed., 2018).
2 Augusto Zimmermann, *Western Legal Theory, Concepts and Perspectives* (LexisNexis Butterworths, 2013) 82.
3 Richard Wasserstrom, 'Lawyers as Professionals: Some Moral Issues' (1975) 5(1) *Human Rights* 1, 12.
4 W Bradley Wendel, *Lawyers and Fidelity to Law* (Princeton University Press, 2010) 85.
5 Wasserstrom, above n 3, 12.

DOI: 10.4324/9781003264286-4

The Role of Lawyers

The principles of a positivist TLE require that 'lawyers have an obligation to regard clients' interests as the most important source of reasons for action', whereas a moral TLE requires lawyers to 'act directly on considerations of ordinary morality'.[6] It is noteworthy that both the moral theorists and positivists use the term 'ordinary morality'. It is used as a general term and not based upon any specific moral philosophy. Nor is ordinary morality related to professional ethics, duties, or any professional role. Rather, ordinary morality involves 'moral principles that apply to us simply as people'.[7] More is at stake, however, than a theory of TLE. Its principles determine how lawyers practise law. Lawyers' professional obligations are influenced by positivist TLE principles because these also define lawyers' role. In this way TLE creates the dynamics of the lawyer-to-client relationship; the trust that the public places in the legal profession; and lawyers' sense of self-worth as legal practitioners.

Lawyers' Role as Political Agents

Every profession has a morality associated with its role. Wendel, a contemporary positivist, says lawyers' role morality is relevant to politics as lawyers are more like 'political officials than ... ordinary moral agents'.[8] Law is derived from law-making in a democracy and that 'the legal system is a political institution that serves indispensable political ends'.[9] The lawyers' role, therefore, is informed by political values and this is where 'the ethical value of lawyering is located' rather than in morality.[10] The institutions and processes comprising our legal system are not isolated from moral and justice concerns,[11] although 'lawyers should not aim directly at justice and should not make decisions in the same way that morally reflective people make any ethical decision'.[12]

Luban, a moral theorist, says that 'Wendel puts too much faith in existing legal institutions and in procedure at the expense of substantive justice'.[13] Kruse identifies Wendel's interpretation of positivist TLE as

---

6 Wendel, above n 4, 105.

7 Ibid., 20.

8 Ibid., 7–8.

9 Ibid., 91.

10 Ibid., 2.

11 Ibid.

12 Ibid., 208.

13 David Luban, 'Misplaced Fidelity' (2012) 90(3) *Texas Law Review* 673, 678.

politics, law's function, and lawyers' role, as a 'theory of democracy justifying a theory of the function of law, which in turn justifies a conception of the lawyer's role'.[14]

Wendel maintains that 'lawyers are not all-purpose agents who facilitate moral deliberation', instead they assist their clients to bring their conduct within legal rights and duties.[15] He is not arguing that lawyers are amoral,[16] just that they are not moral agents in a wider ethical sense, and that ethics is a private matter where all people pursue their moral concerns.[17]

A positivist TLE perspective places politics at the centre as politicians create the law. Therefore, the role of lawyers is to interpret the law and advise clients of their legal rights and obligations. The nexus between politics and the law is further tightened as positivists regard the legal system as a political institution. This casts a narrow compass around politics where lawyers' role is couched in terms of political legitimacy within a legal system that is said to be a political institution. This in turn influences a positivist TLE as it is informed by political values. This explains the positivists' view that lawyers are political officials, not moral agents. Yet, this is far from the reality of much of legal practice. If lawyers can only look to their role as political agents advising upon the law and with ethics being informed by political values, then positivist role morality is not particularly helpful for lawyers. This may explain why researchers are conducting empirical research into the practical effects of a positivist TLE upon lawyers.

In the UK, research demonstrates how the role morality of positivist TLE has been perceived by commercial lawyers. This is relevant because both the UK and Australia have statutory legal ethics[18] and a similar positivist TLE. Vaughan and Oakley, interviewed 57 corporate lawyers from global law firms in the City of London[19] and found lawyers were apathetic about professional ethics.[20] It went further than apathy, extending to a type of 'ethical numbness' (or acquired insensitivity) where lawyers found it difficult

---

14 Katherine Kruse, 'Fidelity to Law and the Moral Pluralism Premise' (2012) 90(3) *Texas Law Review* 657, 657.

15 W Bradley Wendel, 'Legal Ethics Is About the Law, Not Morality or Justice: A Reply to Critics' (2012) 90(3) *Texas Law Review* 727, 732–3.

16 Wendel, above n 4. 7.

17 Ibid., 85.

18 Australia: *Legal Profession Uniform Act 2014* (NSW); UK: Solicitors' Regulation Authority (SRA) Competence Statement A, *Ethics, Professionalism and Judgement,* A1 https://www.sra.org.uk/solicitors/competence-statement.page

19 Steven Vaughan and Emma Oakley, '"Gorilla Exceptions" and the Ethically Apathetic Corporate Lawyer' (2016) 19 *Legal Ethics* 50.

20 Ibid.

to identify any ethical concerns arising in their practice.[21] The researchers linked this to positivist TLE with its 'role morality', including its belief in client supremacy, and lawyers' moral neutrality, as well as lawyers regarding themselves only as technicians of the law.[22] This could reflect a lack of understanding of ethics if lawyers see themselves as nothing more than political agents who view their role morality through that lens. This may also cause lawyers to fail to recognise ethical principles in their professional duties, codes, and statutes.

Lawyers' Role as Moral Agents

Luban says there is a connection between law and morality where 'the rule of law relies on the professional ethics of the lawyers'.[23] He states that moral theorists are motivated in their criticisms of positivist TLE by problems with its role morality.[24] He asks how lawyers' professional role might require them to do things that would be morally forbidden to non-lawyers.[25] He wonders 'why lawyers get a free pass from morality'.[26] This distinguishes the non-lawyer as a person being able to rely upon ethics in their decision-making, whereas lawyers' role morality under positivist TLE removes this option.

Simon agrees with Luban as he finds morality is embodied in the law and that law is actually 'grounded in ordinary morality' with the lawyers' role being connected to it, not separate from it.[27] Luban's own position on positivist TLE is that positivist principles ought to be replaced with moral principles.[28] Generally the role of professionals and their sense of identity is influenced by their moral voice.[29] It, therefore, seems unusual that lawyers' moral voice under positivist TLE is filtered through the lens of politics.

Wasserstrom, writing soon after the Watergate scandal, found that many participants were lawyers. He believed this was not a coincidence but related to the nature of lawyers' role morality that had diminished lawyers'

21 Ibid., 61.
22 Ibid., 50.
23 David Luban, 'Natural Law as Professional Ethics: a Reading of Fuller' (2001) 18(1) *Social Philosophy and Policy* 176, 177.
24 Luban, above n 13, 674.
25 Ibid.
26 Ibid.
27 William Simon, 'Role Differentiation and Lawyers' Ethics: A Critique of Some Academic Perspectives' (2010) 23 *Georgetown Journal of Legal Ethics* 987, 1009.
28 Luban, above n 13, 676.
29 Rachael Field, James Duffy and Anna Huggins, *Lawyering and Positive Professional Identities* (LexisNexis, 2014).

moral considerations.[30] He highlighted the unsatisfactory nature of this role-differentiated behaviour, where it was regarded as appropriate for lawyers to put aside their moral concerns that in other situations would be 'relevant if not decisive'.[31]

Wasserstrom referred to a common criticism that 'the lawyer-client relationship renders the lawyer at best systematically *amoral* and at worst more than occasionally *immoral*'.[32] This criticism indicates detrimental personal consequences for lawyers whose role under a positivist TLE is to give advice with less weight given to moral content. He believed that when lawyers' conduct is attributed to their perceived role, this 'puts the lawyer's integrity into question in a way that distinguishes lawyers from other professionals'.[33] It could also provide a justification for lazy professional ethics as lawyers' role morality is saying to lawyers that their only concern is the law.

The personal cost to lawyers of positivist role morality is that their personal ethics could contradict the ethics embodied in their professional role. This is more than a personal matter of discomfort for lawyers. This also has an impact upon stakeholders affected by lawyers' advice when guided by a positivist TLE. This can enable clients to use the law for unethical purposes as demonstrated in the JH case study. Lawyers cannot prevent clients doing this, but they could give them both legal and ethical advice as developed in the new model of TLE.

Lawyers' Professional Duties and TLE

The importance of TLE is also found in the effect of positivist TLE upon lawyers' professional duties. For example, positivist TLE supports the supremacy of clients. This diminishes lawyers' professional independence and their ability to give the objective advice that is required of them as fiduciaries. Further, lawyers' duty to justice is one of their most important duties[34] but positivists say that lawyers' role does not concern justice directly.[35] Lawyers may suffer moral anxiety because a positivist TLE 'weakens

---

30 Wasserstrom, above n 3, 3.
31 Ibid.
32 Ibid., 1 (emphasis added).
33 Ibid., 14.
34 Dennis Lloyd, *The Idea of Law: A Repressive Evil or Social Necessity?* (Penguin Books, 1981) 117.
35 Wendel, above n 4, 2.

the connection between the practical tasks of lawyering and the values of justice that lawyers believe provide the moral foundations of their role'.[36]

In addition, a positivist TLE 'excessively attenuates the lawyer's responsibility for her [or his] conduct and requires her [or him] to participate in injustice'.[37] Moral philosophers tell us that injustice is unethical.[38] This is a significant objection to positivist TLE, in view of lawyers' duty to justice. Moral theorists make justice a 'central normative touchstone',[39] whereas positivists subordinate it (to law) telling lawyers not to pursue justice directly.[40] Conscientious lawyers may, therefore, follow their profession's TLE resulting in them doing 'things they believe to be unjust'.[41]

The consequences of lawyers being directed by a positivist TLE to concentrate upon the law and not morality too, may be serious from a professional perspective as it could lead to unethical conduct and sometimes illegal conduct by lawyers and their clients. Wasserstrom gave an example of this when he examined the conduct of the Watergate lawyers and found it included: 'lying in public; dissembling; stonewalling; tape-recording conversations; and playing dirty tricks'.[42]

The importance of the deleterious effects of positivist TLE upon lawyers' professional duties is also shown by empirical research in Australia. This demonstrates the influence of positivist TLE upon attitudes and professional practice, here, corporate lawyers in large law firms, and in-house lawyers. The researchers found that these lawyers seemed 'to talk and behave as if they have no right to independent moral judgement'.[43] It was 'not seen as your job to have a moral opinion about your clients' (or employers') activities'.[44] Researchers in the UK reported upon 'the professional ethical consciousness' of in-house and external lawyers, finding they were vulnerable to engagement in conduct that was neither ethical nor legal, in order to satisfy clients.[45]

---

36 William Simon, *The Practice of Justice: A Theory of Lawyers' Ethics* (Harvard University Press, 1998) 2.

37 Ibid., 109.

38 Aristotle, *The Ethics of Aristotle: The Nicomachean Ethics* (J A K Thomson trans., Penguin Books, 1976).

39 William Simon, 'Authoritarian Legal Ethics: Bradley Wendel and the Positivist Turn' (2012) 90(3) *Texas Law Review* 709, 710.

40 Wendel, above n 4, 208.

41 Simon, above n 39, 726.

42 Wasserstrom, above n 3, 11.

43 Parker and Evans, above n 1, 289.

44 Ibid.

45 Moorhead and Hinchly, above n 1, 387.

The Law and Ethics

An historical perspective on the role of law and lawyers assists in understanding why a positivist philosophy underpins TLE. Early legal philosophers argued that law ought to follow natural law theory where law had to be compatible with the 'higher standards of justice and morality'.[46] The relevance of this theory is acknowledged in the way law developed in the West.[47] However, legal thinking upon natural law theory changed in the 19th century with new attitudes to religion and science.[48] Law was regarded as having the objectivity and moral neutrality of science, with law being fully contained within legislation and the law reports.[49] Law would no longer be subject to morality. If law could be perceived objectivity having the moral neutrality of science and be fully contained within legislation and the law reports,[50] then it is understandable that a positivist TLE could separate the law from ethics.

The Separation of Law and Ethics

The first part of positivist TLE views the law and the facts objectively, without reaching a conclusion upon the law's 'justness or merit'.[51] Morality was not a required part of legality[52] and law was morally neutral. Positivists acknowledge the criticisms of this separation.

Moral theorists believe the spirit of the law is added to objective law, as acknowledged in a review of the business practices of Barclays Bank where it was found that the bank had to comply 'with the spirit as well as the letter of prevailing regulation and the law.[53] If lawyers isolate the spirit of the law and its moral content from the law, they may not be able to claim that they are realising law's democratic intent. This then undermines the claim of the political legitimacy of law.[54]

The second part of positivist TLE is found in the three principles, below, that apply to the role of lawyers, the law, morality, and client supremacy.

---

46 Zimmermann, above n 2 1.
47 Ibid.
48 Ibid., 66.
49 Zimmermann, above n 2, 66.
50 Ibid.
51 Ibid., 82.
52 Ibid.
53 Anthony Salz and Russell Collins, 'An Independent Review of Barclays' Business Practices' (Report, April 2013) Anthony Salz, Commissioner ('*Salz Review*') Recommendation 1, 12. http://group.barclays.com/about-barclays/citizenship/salz-review-report
54 Wendel, above n 4, 91.

This part prioritises the interests of clients by putting law at the forefront without consideration of ordinary morality.[55]

- *Principle of Partisanship:* lawyers should seek to advance the interests of clients within the bounds of the law.
- *Principle of Neutrality:* lawyers should not consider the morality of clients' causes, nor the morality of particular actions taken to advance them, as long as both are lawful.
- *Principle of Non-accountability:* if lawyers adhere to the first two principles, neither third-party observers nor lawyers should regard lawyers as wrongdoers, in moral terms.[56]

The first principle suggests that clients' interests may only be advanced if they are within the law. However, clients' interests are broader than that. They could also be advanced by assisting clients to make ethical decisions, a strategy that would preserve the clients' reputations and protect their stakeholders. The second principle narrows the argument to clients' causes irrespective of their morality. Disturbingly, this gives lawyers permission to stand by while clients pursue unethical conduct, if required to advance their cause. The legal profession, and all other professions, contemporaneously represent themselves as practitioners with integrity, and they are, but the contradiction is that positivist TLE will not permit lawyers to give ethical advice.

There is no professional justification for the third principle of moral neutrality and moral non-accountability.[57] Positivist TLE narrows lawyers' perspective to the law and clients' wishes, with no concern for the wider community. This restriction of morality, if not its removal, means that lawyers are forced to contradict their personal morality when they practise law. This, say moral theorists, is difficult to justify. Unlike their clients, lawyers are legal professionals and have personal responsibility for their own professional integrity, a responsibility that cannot be diffused by the morals of clients or their interests and objectives.

Hart, a positivist, maintains that ethics and morality are vague[58] whereas law has the certainty of being comprised of rules.[59] This appears to be a justification for separating the law – which needs certainty – from moral-

---

55 Ibid., 85.
56 Ibid., 6.
57 Wasserstrom, above n 3, 1.
58 H L A Hart, *The Concept of Law* (Clarendon Press, 1982) 164.
59 Ibid., 8.

ity. Morality, however, need not be vague. It is possible to identify moral values and principles. This is what philosophers do. We are also able to bring values and principles into TLE. This is unlikely to affect the certainty of the law given that the 'certainty' of the rules of law is tempered by their interpretation.

Hart admits that 'the law of every modern state shows at a thousand points the influence of both the accepted social morality and wider moral ideals'.[60] However, he says, it does not follow that legal validity must include references to ethics or justice as the law does not necessarily satisfy what morality may demand.[61] Therefore, while acknowledging the influence of morality in the law, legal validity does not depend upon ethical references. The consequence of this is that lawyers have an ethical framework available in the law without the ethical substance of a moral TLE to support it. The distancing of ethics from the law leaves lawyers with nowhere to turn professionally when ethical issues arise.

There are psychological effects upon lawyers of the separation of law and ethics in positivist TLE. Simon, a moral theorist, worries that viewing the law as objective, while moral obligation is on the periphery and subjective, 'implies that the lawyer who adopts [a moral obligation] is on his or her own and vulnerable both intellectually and practically'.[62] There is a psychological bias in favour of positivist TLE because the effect of its focus upon the law, without moral obligation, makes it psychologically more difficult for the legal profession and students to argue for a moral conception.[63]

Fidelity to the Law

Wendel proposed a new version of positivist TLE that includes fidelity to, or respect for, the law as 'the fundamental ethical obligation of lawyers'.[64] He says this new version of positivist TLE[65] arises from 'a conceptual wrong turn' made by positivist TLE when it tries to rely upon 'ordinary ethics to address the problems of lawyers'.[66] Wendel urges lawyers to refocus upon the law and the clients.[67] This appears to be an acknowledgement that posi-

---

60 Ibid., 199.

61 Ibid., 181.

62 William Simon, 'Should Lawyers Obey the Law?' (1996) 38(1) *William and Mary Law Review* 217, 247.

63 Ibid.

64 Wendel, above n 4, 89.

65 Wendel, above n 4, 6.

66 Ibid., 7–8.

67 Ibid., 85.

tivist TLE puts lawyers in a difficult position as they cannot address ethical issues when they encounter them in legal practice. This may be why lawyers are trying to rely upon ordinary ethics. If so, this would support the argument that positivist TLE is no longer suitable for lawyers.

Kruse says Wendel's new TLE comprises two arguments, one being *functional* and the other *normative*.[68] She maintains that both arguments concern *respect*[69] for the law. The functional argument is that 'law deserves respect even from those who disagree with its substantive justice ... because law establishes a stable framework'.[70] The normative argument is that 'the law is entitled to respect because the democratic lawmaking processes through which it is enacted, respect the equality and dignity of citizens'.[71] Further, the law has to provide a reason why society should respect it and this must be 'strong enough to trump the moral reasons to avoid law's reach'.[72] If the community perceives a decision is incorrect and by implication the law is wrong as it offends morality, then respect for the law has to be deep enough to counter moral concerns. If not, the law will be brought into disrepute.

Fidelity to law does not need to be limited to respect for the law's authority, which Kruse says is 'settled according to thin procedural standards of adequate fairness'.[73] Luban comments that 'fidelity to law is a virtue', and conscience is separate from fidelity.[74] Further 'the legal system works best ... if people keep their conscience switched on'.[75]

The principles of positivist TLE do not offer the depth of ethical content that legal professional ethics requires in the 21st century. Rules, such as those provided by the law, are always subject to principles of interpretation and these principles are most likely to be informed by social ideals such as ethics. It is argued that it is ethics that gives both law and professional ethics their meaning.

The Role of Ethics in Legal Practice

We saw in the JH case study what happens when ethical issues are not addressed. They can have serious consequences for clients and their stakeholders. Appeals by lawyers to the principle of equality before the law, and

---

68 Kruse, above n 14, 660 (emphasis in original).
69 Ibid., (emphasis in original).
70 Ibid.
71 Ibid.
72 Ibid., 663.
73 Ibid., 671.
74 Luban, above n 13, 690.
75 Luban, above n 13, 688.

the source of law's creation by democratically elected representatives, do not provide ethical answers for lawyers. A theoretical position that separates law and ethics is on its face, difficult to justify when this refers to professional practice and accountability of lawyers in matters of ethical substance. What immediately comes to mind is lawyers' professional integrity which one would think should be supported by ethics within TLE.

Positivists are aware of the different ethical perspectives of a positivist and a moralist TLE. Wendel admits 'philosophers would be baffled to hear lawyers say things like: "That may be unethical, but it isn't wrong"'.[76] In other words, 'wrong' is only that which offends positivist TLE such as a breach of law. Unethical decisions are not 'wrong' according to a positivist TLE. It is disturbing that this distancing of ethics from the law represents a significant part of positivist TLE.

Perhaps the better approach to address these shortcomings in a positivist TLE, is the argument that the distance between ethics and the law needs to be closed, preferably by a moral model of TLE. This will assist clients and their stakeholders primarily but also lawyers who will be seen to be acting with professional integrity, especially when the public believes that professionals are supposed to be examples of ethical conduct.[77]

The Role of Ethics in Lawyers' Advice

An important example of ethical conduct in legal practice would be if lawyers could give their clients ethical (as well as legal) advice. Unlike positivist TLE, the new moral model of TLE is a template for lawyers to guide them in the process. Firstly, to identify ethical issues in clients' instructions by application of the moral philosophies of Aristotle and Kant, see Chapter 5; then to undertake moral reasoning to enable ethical advice to be formulated. Clients may not wish to follow ethical advice. It is their choice. The argument is that lawyers ought to have a model of legal ethics that specifies that as professionals they are required to give both ethical and legal advice to clients.

Another consideration is whether lawyers have the expertise or competence to offer ethical advice. They are not ethicists or philosophers, but they do not make this representation. Lawyers already have knowledge of some ethical concepts in their professional obligations, such as acting in the interests of justice, professional integrity, and upholding their clients' trust. The

---

76 Wendel, above n 4, 19.

77 Clancy Martin, Wayne Vaught and Robert C Solomon, *Ethics Across the Professions: a Reader for Professional Ethics* (Oxford University Press, 2010) 2.

concepts of justice and integrity are further developed by Aristotle's moral virtues, whereas Kantian ethics refers to our duties to others, such as clients, and maintaining their trust. The new moral model of TLE, in Chapter 7, enables lawyers to give ethical advice as competent lawyers with enough knowledge of ethical principles to assist clients to make ethical decisions that may flow from lawyers' legal and ethical advice.

Wendel's new version of positivist TLE, permits lawyers to assist clients when giving advice, to realise only their legal entitlements and not the broader clients' interests.[78] Under positivist TLE, clients' interests include both legal and commercial interests.[79] Wendel reiterated that positivist TLE requires lawyers not to consider ordinary morality.[80] He acknowledges that this is a barren ethical position for lawyers if ordinary morality is not there to constrain lawyers, as they will be left with nothing but the pursuit of clients' interests.[81] He argued that there is no *moral* obligation for lawyers to counsel their clients on the basis of what the spirit of the law requires because clients have only a *legal* obligation to obey the law, not a moral obligation.[82] We might consider whether we have a moral obligation not to use the law for unethical purposes. The JH case study showed how this occurs. Here JH used the law to restructure the group, transferring assets from Amaca and Amaba to MRCF, and positivist TLE did not permit JH's lawyers to give ethical advice. The result was that when MRCF's funds were depleted, tort claimants were left without a remedy.

Pepper's response to Wendel's new version of TLE, shows the nature of lawyers' advice and ethical and legal practice. Pepper says that if lawyers were limited in their advice to only legal obligations of clients, as Wendel suggests, this would prohibit '*much of the stretching and manipulation currently found ethically acceptable in the practice of law*'.[83] Luban appears to acknowledge this practice as he says lawyers need to rely upon ordinary morality otherwise 'the law may be so manipulable that an obligation of fidelity to law is inherently unworkable'.[84] Pepper's revelation of what is regarded as 'ethical' legal practice appears to support the concerns of moral theorists.

78 Wendel, above n 4, 6.
79 Ibid.
80 Ibid., 85.
81 Ibid., 12–13.
82 Ibid., 105 (emphasis in original).
83 Stephen L Pepper, 'The Lawyer Knows More than the Law' (2012) 90(3) *Texas Law Review* 691, 692 (emphasis added).
84 David Luban, *Lawyers and Justice: An Ethical Study* (Princeton University Press, 1988) 16.

Pepper and Wendel disagree about offering moral advice to clients. Pepper thinks that lawyers need to be: 'held responsible for ensuring that the client knows there is, in the lawyer's opinion, a gap between law and justice' and that the client is 'responsible for injustice if it occurs'.[85] Wendel says the lawyer-to-client relationship is similar to a relationship between strangers.[86] Pepper disputes this stating that lawyers are close to 'morally wrongful conduct and consequences – and directly facilitative of it' and this is not a relationship between strangers.[87] Significantly Pepper says if positivist TLE regards the lawyer-to-client relationship as one between strangers, then clients may use this to separate themselves from arguably wrongful conduct and say that their lawyers or the law is responsible for it.[88]

The possibility of making lawyers responsible for their clients' wrong-doing should concern all lawyers. This is a powerful reason to support a new moral TLE. Clients need to be held responsible for any decisions they make that may cause injustice, provided lawyers advise them beforehand that injustice is a likely outcome. Rhode, a moral theorist, says that lawyers have a '*personal* responsibility for the consequences of professional acts'.[89] Presumably this includes their professional advice and if lawyers include a warning in their advice to clients that injustice may be an outcome of clients' decisions, then this would absolve lawyers of personal responsibility, but not the clients.

Vischer, a moral theorist, says the absence of morality in positivist TLE has given lawyers the role of 'amoral technicians'.[90] He acknowledges that prominent theorists in positivist TLE have tried to address this by appeals to client autonomy,[91] client loyalty,[92] and political legitimacy[93] but none of these appeals considers the 'extra-legal conceptions of morality'[94] that envisage a moral

---

85 Stephen L Pepper, 'Lawyers' Ethics in the Gap Between Law and Justice' (1999) 40 *Texas Law Review* 181, 190.

86 Wendel, above n 4, 142.

87 Pepper, above n 83, 699.

88 Ibid., 702.

89 Deborah Rhode, *In the Interests of Justice: Reforming the Legal Profession* (Oxford University Press, 2000) 17 (emphasis added).

90 Robert Vischer, 'Legal Advice as Moral Perspective' (2006) 19 *Georgetown Journal of Legal Ethics* 225, 228.

91 Stephen L Pepper, 'The Lawyer's Amoral Ethical Role: A Defense, a Problem, and Some Possibilities, (1986)11 *American Bar Foundation Research Journal* 613.

92 Charles Fried, 'The Lawyer as Friend: The Moral Foundation of the Lawyer-Client Relation' (1976) 85 *Yale Law Journal* 1060.

93 Wendel, above n 4.

94 Vischer, above n 90, 228.

dialogue between lawyers and their clients.[95] Vischer examines lawyers' professional moral perspective that derives from 'values and priorities of lawyering' such as 'secrecy, defensiveness, and rights-maximization, with [the minimization of] qualities like compassion, vulnerability, and risk-taking'.[96]

Client Supremacy

The positivist TLE principle of client supremacy tells lawyers to prioritise clients and their legal and commercial interests.[97] Wendel's new version of positivist TLE narrows this to clients' legal entitlements.[98]

Client Supremacy and Lawyers' Professional Duties

Client supremacy may cause lawyers to lose their professional autonomy. They could find it difficult to make the objective and independent judgements they need to fulfil their duties to the court, the administration of justice, and as fiduciaries.[99] Once this autonomy is lost, lawyers may not easily distinguish their arguments for their clients from their own independent opinions on 'what the law is or ought to be'.[100]

Lawyers' duties to the court and justice are key duties for the profession, yet client supremacy advances clients' interests and a right to a narrow focus upon legal rules, even if this 'leads to injustice for others'.[101] The duty to justice is a public duty that takes priority to clients. Former Chief Justice Mason, High Court of Australia, stated that 'the duty to the court is paramount and must be performed, even if the client gives instructions to the contrary'.[102]

Lawyers' fiduciary duty is a private duty where lawyers should give independent advice in the clients' best interests. However, clients may propose to engage in misleading conduct using the argument that this is acceptable business practice, although its lawfulness is debatable. If lawful it would not breach

---

95 Ibid., 230.
96 Ibid.
97 Wendel, above n 4, 6.
98 Ibid., 52.
99 G E Dal Pont, *Lawyers' Professional Responsibility* (Thomson Reuters, 7th ed., 2021) [17.10] 570.
100 Richard L Abel and Philip S C Lewis, 'Putting Law Back into the Sociology of Lawyers' in Richard L Abel and Philip S C Lewis (eds), *Lawyers in Society, vol 3, Comparative Theories* (University of California Press, 1989) 281, 503.
101 Simon, above n 36, 26.
102 *Giannarelli v Wraith* (1988) 165 CLR 543, 556.

the principles of positivist TLE. Lawyers could assert their independence by advising the proposed action is not in the clients' best interests, it being 'tricky' conduct that is unethical and could damage the clients' business and personal reputations. This would require lawyers to refute client supremacy which they cannot do under positivist TLE. Alternatively, it could be argued by lawyers that their failure to advise clients that clients' proposed action is not in their best interests, is a breach of their fiduciary duty.

This is the dilemma for positivist TLE. Lawyers' professional autonomy is diminished in favour of client supremacy, but this comes at a cost for clients. They are better served if lawyers give both legal and ethical advice, that each is part of clients' best interests. Wendel's new version of positivist TLE proposes a restructure of the lawyer to client relationship as 'the ideal of fidelity to *law*, not to clients', where lawyers are guided by the 'legal and ethical ideals of fiduciary obligations'.[103] This comes close to accepting that lawyers ought to give ethical advice to clients.

Client Supremacy and Legal Practice

Client supremacy under a positivist TLE may produce bizarre outcomes for lawyers. An example is the legal advice given to the Bush Administration by government lawyers in the Office of Legal Counsel, US Department of Justice. Legal counsel were asked to advise whether the treatment of suspected terrorists in Iraq's Abu Ghraib prison was torture, as this was illegal under both US domestic and international law.

The advice concluded that the interrogation techniques, although appearing to be torture, were not. They were, therefore, legal. Leaked memoranda from the Office of Legal Counsel revealed that 'these lawyers engaged in jurisprudential gymnastics in an effort to validate the sort of practices that had sparked worldwide revulsion'.[104] This unethical outcome did not reflect well upon the advice itself, nor upon the legal profession. The White House later distanced itself from the advice of its own lawyers.[105] Vischer said this advice revealed that 'the legal profession lacks discernible moral resources … to condemn' these attorneys for their behaviour and he regarded legal ethics as a 'distinctly uninspiring vision of lawyers as amoral technicians.'[106]

This demonstrates the unfortunate consequences that may result from positivists' narrow focus upon the law and clients with ethical issues being

---

103   Wendel, above n 4, 168 (emphasis added).
104   Ibid.
105   Ibid., 226.
106   Ibid., 228.

sidestepped. A positivist TLE is unsatisfactory, as this model may create a professional abyss for lawyers where they could find themselves giving advice that is as difficult to justify as it is morally abhorrent to them personally and to the community more broadly.

Tim Dare, a positivist, stated that there is near unanimity that a positivist TLE should no longer be supported when duties to clients 'allow and perhaps even require conduct that would otherwise be morally impermissible'.[107]Dare acknowledges that critics observe that positivist TLE 'requires excessive and immoral advocacy on behalf of clients'.[108] He supports zealous, not hyper-zealous lawyers where the former are 'concerned solely with the legal interests of clients.[109]

Deborah Rhode, a moral theorist, identified the problem for corporate lawyers created by client supremacy. She says lawyers may be in a position where they give legal advice upon 'socially indefensible' but 'technically legal' conduct where prohibition is too expensive or 'decision-making bodies are uninformed'[110] of likely detrimental consequences. She says that a positivist TLE with its emphasis upon law and client demands has resulted in some of the 'most socially costly enterprises in recent memory', for example: the health effects of mining and the use of asbestos; and the suppression of health information about tobacco use (particularly) in cigarettes'.[111]

Charles Fried, a positivist, asked an important question that has resonated with lawyers over the decades ever since, and this is whether a good lawyer could also be a good person.[112] This question continues to be an important 'challenge to the foundations of legal ethics'.[113] Fried was concerned that the client-centred approach under client supremacy leads to 'the willingness of lawyers to help their clients use the law to the prejudice of the weak or the innocent' which he says 'seems morally corrupt'.[114] Loyalty to clients, and the view of the lawyer as the client's friend 'does account for a kind of callousness towards society and exclusively in the service of

---

107 Tim Dare, 'Mere-Zeal, Hyper-Zeal and the Ethical Obligations of Lawyers' (2004) 7(1) *Legal Ethics* 24, 24.

108 Ibid.

109 Ibid., 30.

110 Deborah Rhode, 'Ethics in Practice' in D Rhode (ed.), *Ethics in Practice: Lawyers' Roles Responsibilities and Regulation* (Oxford University Press, 2000) 10.

111 Ibid.

112 Fried, above n 92, 1060.

113 Christine Parker, 'The Philosophical Foundations of Legal Ethics: a Roundtable' in Kieran Tranter *et al* (eds) *Reaffirming Legal Ethics: Taking Stock and New Ideas* (Routledge, 2010) 12.

114 Fried, above n 92, 1060.

the client'.[115] This conduct may have psychological implications too for the lawyers as they, like all of us, want to believe that we behave ethically and that we are 'good, worthwhile individuals'.[116]

The James Hardie Case and Positivist TLE

In the JH case study, the client James Hardie Industries Ltd (JHIL), was in a strong position commercially in relation to both the tort victims and its lawyers. The client's actions were prejudicial to the vulnerable tort victims. The commercial strategies JHIL adopted to protect itself from financial risk resulted in insufficient compensation for victims. The principles of positivist TLE are applied here to decisions Allens, external lawyers, and its response to ethical issues arising from their relationship with client, JHIL.

Principle of Partisanship

This principle may restrict the professionalism of lawyers by diminishing their independence and narrowing the scope of lawyers' role. Professionally, lawyers are meant to be independent and look beyond clients to their duties: the administration of justice,[117] the public interest,[118] and their own integrity.

Advancing Client, JHIL's, Interests within the Law

The client's interests were to enable the fulfilment of the group subsidiaries' legal obligations under tort law: compensation for tort victim employees for the effects of asbestos exposure. The required funding for tort liabilities had to be ascertained. Numerous tactics were used by JHIL to protect itself, as parent company, from having to pay compensation. For example, there were few checks on funding requirements.

Allens, external lawyers, advanced JHIL's interest. It appears it did not challenge JHIL's calculation of tort liabilities; instead, accepting JHIL's assurances that funding provisions were adequate. Allens did not consider the morality of the client's actions as they are not required to do so under positivist TLE. Lawyers advance client interests as identified by the client.

---

115 Ibid., 1087.

116 Donald Langevoort, 'Where Were the Lawyers? A Behavioral Inquiry into Lawyers' Responsibility for Clients' Fraud' (1993) 48 *Vanderbilt Law Review* 75, 103.

117 Dal Pont, above n 99, [17.10) 570.

118 William Sullivan, *Work and Integrity: the Crisis and Promise of Professionalism in America* (Jossey=Bass, 2nd ed., 2005) 23.

This is encouraged by the principle of partisanship and client supremacy. This dissuades lawyers from making their own independent assessment.

Professional Independence

The client, JHIL, did not incorporate current actuarial data when it calculated the tort liabilities, although funding arrangements for the Medical Research and Compensation Foundation (MRCF) depended upon this. JHIL's group counsel, Peter Shafron, assured Allens that the most recent data were not required.[119] Commissioner Jackson said advisors knew that the funding had 'to be rigorously checked', but he acknowledged JHIL did not welcome 'outside advice' on this matter.[120]Client-centred legal ethics encouraged Allens to accept JHIL's assurances.

Justice and the Public Good

The funding of MRCF by JHIL was later shown to fall short of requirements, resulting in many tort victims receiving no compensation at all. It is not in the public good to have these stakeholders unjustly denied remediation. However, this is not a breach of positivist TLE because it is beyond the scope of TLE to consider matters of injustice and ethical consequence. It is within positivist TLE to consider the public good, it is just an impoverished version of the public good. These issues were devastating for tort victims and damaging to JHIL's reputation.

Moral Neutrality: Lawyers Consider Neither the Morality of the Client's Cause Nor Actions Taken to Advance it, if within the Law

The Morality of the Client's Cause

The tortfeasor subsidiary companies, Amaba and Amaca, were owned by JHIL whose cause was to increase the group's profit by minimising the tort liability of these companies, isolating this liability, ending JHIL's financial risk, if any, and providing unverified funding to MRCF. This was immoral as victims were vulnerable people who would suffer from a funding shortfall,

---

119 *Australian Securities and Investments Commission v Macdonald (No 11)* [2009] NSWSC 287 [328] 105–6.

120 New South Wales, 'Special Commission of Inquiry into the Medical Research and Compensation Foundation' (Report, September 2004) David Jackson QC, Commissioner ('*Jackson Report*') [29.14–15] 547. https://www.dpc.nsw.gov.au/publications/categories

but positivist TLE tells lawyers that they cannot consider morality. The cause was legal and under positivist TLE that was all that mattered.

The Morality of Actions to Advance Client Causes

The restructure was used by JHIL to advance its cause. This resulted in a transfer of JHIL's ownership of the subsidiary companies to MRCF which would now be legally liable to meet tort claims.[121] If MRCF were not sufficiently funded it would not be able to meet all claims. This was the ethical issue.

The restructure was approved by the Supreme Court in August 2001 with a major financial protection for tort victims worth A$1.9billion,[122] whereby JHIL could later call upon JHI NV's partly paid shares to pay part or all of the remaining issue price.[123] Nevertheless, by 2003 MRCF had revealed its assets would be depleted in four to five years resulting in *80 per cent of future victims being unlikely to have their claims considered let alone met.*[124]

The worsening funding position of MRCF revealed the necessity of the protection offered by the partly paid shares. Santow J, of the Supreme Court, had been given assurances by JHIL and Allens that these funds were there to protect tort victims.[125] The restructure was approved. Eighteen months later, however, the shares were cancelled, which although within the law, effectively removed the premise upon which approval had been given. A positivist TLE could not address the ethical issue of removing the promised protection for tort victims.

Commissioner Jackson found that both JHIL and Allens had contravened their legal duties 'of disclosure in the proceedings before Santow J' in relation to these shares, although the Commissioner found this was unintentional.[126] This illegality meant that Allens was in breach of a crucial requirement of positivist TLE: legal compliance. The circumstances of the partly paid shares demonstrate that where TLE is client-centred, lawyers may rely too readily and completely upon client assurances attributing a degree of veracity to those assurances that may not exist.

---

121 Ibid., [27.22] 8.
122 Ibid., [25.17–25.18] 429.
123 Ibid., [25.5] 423.
124 Ibid., [27.22] 496 (emphasis added).
125 Ibid., [25.37] 436.
126 Ibid., [25.91] 456 (emphasis added).

Non-Accountability: Lawyers Are Not Wrongdoers in Moral Terms, When Following TLE Principles

Positivist philosophy does a disservice to lawyers by removing morality and moral accountability from TLE. Although TLE requires lawyers and clients to uphold the law, paradoxically positivist TLE may create an environment in which the law is breached by both lawyers and clients. This occurred in the JH case when they each contravened their duty of disclosure.

If client interests are unethical, they cannot be addressed by positivist TLE and nor are lawyers accountable for not doing so. Positivist TLE diminishes professional and personal independence, yet lawyers need both to make professional judgements that require *moral partiality,* not moral neutrality, to guide them in legal practice. Perversely, as seen in examples above, positivist TLE sometimes leads to breaches of the law, thereby diminishing *legal* compliance, the very issue that positivist TLE has at its core.

Conclusion

Theoretical legal ethics is important as it influences how lawyers practise law including their interpretation of it, their professional duties, and their relationship with clients. Ultimately lawyers' TLE specifies principles that inform lawyers' professional role and the scope of their advice to clients.

Positivist TLE could result in lawyers engaging in convoluted arguments to justify this model's separation of law and ethics. Moral theorists understand the importance positivist TLE attributes to lawyers upholding their legal duty to the law. It is the separation of ethics from the law that concerns them. Add to this the positivist TLE's first principle of partisanship – client supremacy – that encourages lawyers to adhere to client demands (within the law). Positivist TLE then becomes a barren ground for lawyers restricted to anything clients may want, if it is possible and within the law. This impinges upon lawyers' important professional attributes: namely, the ability to act independently of clients, giving objective advice, and acting in the interests of justice and with integrity.

Positivist TLE's second principle, moral neutrality, prevents lawyers considering the morality of the client's cause (within the law). This also narrows lawyers' professional role to doing what clients demand and not advising upon associated moral issues. Positivist TLE's third principle says lawyers are not morally accountable for the effects of principles one and two. Moral non-accountability does not sit well with the professional integrity that lawyers are expected to uphold. This is exacerbated by the public and stakeholders' failure to comprehend lawyers' apparent involvement in giving advice and engaging a legal process to realise clients' immoral decisions. These are the costs to lawyers professionally and personally of positivist TLE.

Ultimately positivist TLE is an indication of how the legal profession identifies itself. If lawyers adopted the vision of moral theorists and included morals in a new TLE, this would enhance lawyers' professional integrity and provide a moral vision for legal practice in the 21st century.

Chapter 5 builds upon this conclusion as it examines which moral principles would be most suitable to include in a new TLE. This chapter analyses the moral philosophies of John Stuart Mill,[127] Aristotle,[128] and Kant.[129] Each philosophy has a different perspective that might be a moral guide for transactional lawyers when exercising their professional obligations.

---

127 Richard De George, *Business Ethics* (Prentice Hall, 7th ed., 2010) 44.
128 Aristotle, above n 38.
129 Immanuel Kant, *Foundations of the Metaphysics of Morals* (Lewis White Beck trans., Bobbs-Merrill, 1978).

5   Legal Ethics and Moral Philosophy

The public trust lawyers to use their expertise in the best interests of clients and, indirectly, for the public good. There is a perception that lawyers' professional ethics, as the name suggests, includes ethics. Lawyers could make this perception a reality by including moral principles in legal ethics and thus rekindle deserved esteem for the legal profession.

Theoretical legal ethics (TLE) and professional obligations are the two limbs of lawyers' legal ethics. Each limb ought to be complementary. Both require moral principles to truly serve lawyers in the practice of law in the 21st century, yet only one limb, professional obligations, has ethical principles within it. If the other limb, theoretical legal ethics, included ethics too, it would remove the contradiction that presently exists between the two limbs. Moral philosophy could provide the ethical principles needed to support each part of legal ethics. The philosophies that best assist legal practice are Aristotle's virtue ethics,[1] and Kant's duty ethics.[2] John Stuart Mill's utilitarian ethics[3] is less suitable for professionals, as explained below.

An Overview of Three Moral Philosophies

Aristotelian philosophy, known as virtue ethics, concerns character that is informed by moral virtues, including honesty, courage, and empathy.[4] These are combined with intellectual virtues such as rationality and knowledge.[5]

---

1 Aristotle, *The Ethics of Aristotle: The Nicomachean Ethics* (J A K Thomson trans., Penguin Books, 1976).
2 Immanuel Kant, *Foundations of the Metaphysics of Morals* (Lewis White Beck trans., Bobbs-Merrill 1978).
3 Richard De George, *Business Ethics* (Prentice Hall, 7th ed., 2010) 44.
4 Aristotle, above n 1, 90.
5 Ibid.

DOI: 10.4324/9781003264286-5

Both categories of virtues support the integrity and practical wisdom[6] required by lawyers to make ethical judgements in their clients' matters.

Kantian philosophy, known as duty ethics, argues that we have duties to others that arise from universal moral laws.[7] These duties: to assist vulnerable persons, honesty, respect of persons, and treating people as ends in themselves rather than a means to an end.[8] These three duties also constitute the moral foundation for lawyers' fiduciary duty to clients.

Utilitarian philosophy's ethical goal is to produce the best outcomes for as many people affected by a decision as possible.[9] Utilitarians say that the ethicality of a decision is established by examining its consequences and that 'actions by themselves have no intrinsic value'.[10] Rather, their 'moral value' occurs only when we think about the outcomes of decisions,[11] calculated by weighing up their positive and negative consequences for each stakeholder group.[12] An ethical decision is one where there are positive outcomes for a majority of stakeholders in a group,[13] and also positive outcomes in a majority of stakeholder groups.

Utilitarian philosophy's contribution to lawyers' core obligations of professional integrity and to the duty to justice, may be very small indeed. This philosophy's criteria essentially concern how stakeholders of decisions are affected. Lawyers as professionals cannot engage in these calculations as they may lead them to violate their professional duties, codes, and statutory obligations. The criteria in utilitarian moral philosophy are not relevant to lawyers' professional integrity, concepts of justice, or other duties as no duty relies upon majorities. These are important reasons for not including the utilitarian philosophy's principles in legal ethics. The moral philosophies of Aristotle and Kant are complementary and together they more clearly promote the high moral standard that society expects of lawyers.

The Moral Philosophy of Aristotle

Aristotle's study of virtue ethics in *Nicomachean Ethics* remains influential today[14] and is widely regarded as one of the most important moral phi-

---

6 Ibid., 222.
7 Kant, above n 2, 50–1.
8 Ibid., 45–7.
9 Laura P Hartman, Joseph DesJardins, Chris MacDonald, *Business Ethics: Decision Making for Personal Integrity and Social Responsibility* (McGraw Hill, 5th ed., 2021) 64.
10 De George, above n 3, 44.
11 Ibid.
12 Ibid., 45.
13 De George, above n 3, 46.
14 Aristotle, above n 1.

losophies.[15] Aristotle believed that character development was the way to achieve ethical conduct, as persons of good character will have the moral fortitude and intellectual powers to make ethical decisions.[16]

The Importance of Character

Virtue ethics asks: 'What kind of person should I be?', 'How should I lead my life in order to be a person of good character?'.[17] Virtue ethics also asks: 'What are the prominent moral issues in a situation?'.[18] This latter question is answered by virtue ethicists' recourse to one's own character.[19] Good character is important for lawyers too. It is a prerequisite for admission to legal practice by the Supreme Court. A prospective lawyer has to be 'a fit and proper person to be admitted to the Australian legal profession'.[20] In addition, practising lawyers are required to maintain 'the integrity of legal services'.[21]

Aristotle argues that all our conduct and knowledge are regarded as pursuing the goal of a good.[22] Further, that it is a 'greater and more perfect thing to achieve' good for a community rather than self.[23] This important distinction reveals good character has a greater purpose than the individual. Aristotle's words reflect the major focus of all moral philosophy: going beyond self-interest to consider the wider perspective of community benefit[24] which indirectly also serves self-interest as individuals share in community benefits. What then, is an action or pursuit that is 'good'? Aristotle refers to 'moral goodness',[25] ... 'an activity of soul in accordance with virtue'.[26]

Good character is relevant to lawyers' professional duties that first and foremost address the proper operation of the legal system and justice for the public good. Although lawyers as fiduciaries act in the interests

---

15 Jonathan Barnes, 'Introduction' in Aristotle, *The Ethics of Aristotle: The Nicomachean Ethics* (J A K Thomson, trans., Penguin Books, 1976) 9.

16 James Urmson, *Aristotle's Ethics* (Blackwell Publishers, 1988) 27.

17 Stan van Hooft, *Understanding Virtue Ethics* (Acumen Publishing Ltd, 2006) 11.

18 Ibid.

19 Ibid.

20 *Legal Profession Uniform Law Act 2014* (NSW) s 17(1)(c).

21 Ibid., s 126(a).

22 Aristotle, above n 1, 63.

23 Ibid., 64.

24 Damian Grace and Stephen Cohen, *Business Ethics* (Oxford University Press, 5th ed., 2013) 6.

25 Aristotle, above n 1, 87.

26 Ibid., 76.

of clients, they also have the broader responsibility to act for the public good. When clients' interests contradict community interest, lawyers have both a professional and an ethical problem. Character development as proposed by Aristotle could add to lawyers' ability to resolve professional and ethical issues.

Virtues and Excellence

There are two distinct aspects of 'excellence of action': character, and the thinking that 'controls our choices'.[27] These lead to a fundamental question for Aristotle, namely: What sort of character is needed if sound choices are to be made?[28] Aristotelians value excellence as it enables us to flourish and to meet our moral duties to others.[29] Aristotle believed that ethical conduct could be achieved from within, and that our character will help us make ethical decisions.[30]

Excellence too is a requirement for the legal profession. This begins with many years of tertiary education and continues into legal practice. A condition of the annual renewal of lawyers' practising certificates is to update legal knowledge each year by undertaking units of study prescribed by the Law Society, the lawyers' professional body.[31]

Intellectual and Moral Virtues

Character development requires both our intellectual and moral virtues (such as courage and honesty).[32] There is a close connection between intellectual and moral virtues. The intellect, not our emotions, requires us to examine the right principle to direct our search for the relevant moral virtue, and this is a matter of rational choice.[33]

Aristotle distinguishes the sources of virtues. Intellectual virtues are created by the acquisition of knowledge and take time to develop,[34] whereas moral virtues are concerned with what we feel and what we do.[35] Moral

---

27 Urmson, above n 16, 21–2.
28 Ibid., 22.
29 Ibid.
30 Aristotle, above n 1, 90.
31 Law Society of New South Wales, Continuing Professional Development Program (CPD) https://www.lawsociety.com.au/CPD
32 Aristotle, above n 1, 90.
33 Ibid., 117–18.
34 Ibid., 91.
35 Ibid., 101 (emphasis added).

virtues are not part of our nature,[36] although nature enables us to use them.[37] Habit plays a significant role for Aristotle, as he says that the full development of our moral virtues is the result of habit and we learn when we engage in conduct and repeat or habituate it.[38]

Aristotle and Our Choices

Aristotle prioritises the intellectual virtues when determining ethical conduct. He shows that our intellect examines the right principle[39] as 'purposive reasoning' and this is 'the origin of choice'.[40] Our actions originate from our choices.[41] Rational choices influence the development of the moral virtues within us and in what we perceive as good.[42] If the outcome is what we perceive is good conduct, we then habituate our choices – thus further developing our virtues.[43]

Aristotle's central theme is the power of habit and its influence upon our conduct. He urges us to carefully choose what we do, as our actions shape our character.[44] Further, if we make poor choices and habituate them, it may be very difficult to change our behaviour. Even if we desire to break a habit, it may be too late.[45]

Practical Wisdom

Aristotle shows something more is required of us. This is practical wisdom, or prudence, as it enables us to make a judgement upon the most appropriate virtues for the situation.[46] Prudence links the moral and intellectual virtues.[47] The role of prudence is important as it is this 'virtue that glues the other moral virtues together'.[48] Prudence is also relevant to lawyers when

---

36 Ibid., 91.
37 Ibid.
38 Ibid.
39 Ibid., 117–18.
40 Ibid., 205.
41 Ibid.
42 Ibid., 117–18.
43 Ibid., 91.
44 Ibid., 123.
45 Ibid., 124.
46 Ibid., 222.
47 Ibid.
48 Michael Macaulay and Surendra Arjoon, 'An Aristotelian-Thomistic Approach to Professional Ethics' (2013) 16(2) *Journal of Markets and Morality* 507, 518.

they make a judgement relying upon 'a combination of experience, virtues, values, and knowledge' to advise their clients.[49]

The Moral Philosophy of Immanuel Kant

A study of Kant's philosophy begins with his *Foundations of the Metaphysics of Morals* that explores 'the foundations of *man's duties and rights'*.[50] Kant remains a central figure in Western philosophy.[51] He proposed that universal moral laws apply to all of us and that we owe duties to others that arise from these laws.[52] Kantians ask: 'What action must I take to fulfil my moral duty to others?'.[53] Kantian philosophy is about others. Contrast this with Aristotelian philosophy that asks: 'What kind of person should I be?'. This is a question about self. However, both philosophies are about making ethical decisions in relation to others.

The Importance of Reason

Reason is at the core of Kantian philosophy as Kant wants to identify how we, as human beings, formulate moral judgement to make moral decisions.[54] Kant's idea is that the foundations of our duties are sought 'in the concepts of pure reason'.[55] The high standard of conduct required to fulfil a duty is predicated upon purity of reasoning as only this satisfies that standard.

Interestingly, Kant then considers some of the Aristotelian virtues. While Kant acknowledges the intellectual virtue of intelligence and the moral virtue of courage, he regards these as insufficient because he wonders what our will is likely to do with these virtues.[56] Kant argues that virtues are capable of being used to engage in either good or harmful conduct and the determining factor is our will because it decides how these virtues will be used.[57] For example, Kant says the virtues of courage and perseverance are gifts of nature but if our will, which he also calls character, is not

---

49 Stephen Pepper, 'Three Dichotomies in Lawyers' Ethics: (With Particular Attention to the Corporation as Client)' (2015) 28 *The Georgetown Journal of Legal Ethics* 1069, 1103.
50 Kant, above n 2 (emphasis in original).
51 Lewis White Beck, translator of Immanuel Kant, *Foundations of the Metaphysics of Morals* (Bobbs-Merrill, 1978) Introduction, viii.
52 Kant, above n 2, 20 (Kant's First Section).
53 Van Hooft, above n 17, 10–11.
54 Claus Dierksmeier, 'Kant on Virtue' (2013) 113 *Journal of Business Ethics* 597, 600.
55 Kant, above n 2, preface, 6.
56 Ibid., 11.
57 Ibid.

good then these virtues may be used to harm others.[58] Kantian ethics see a correlation of virtues and duties where 'the proper path to virtue is the fulfilment of our duties'.[59]

Universal Moral Laws and the Categorical Imperative

The role of universal moral law is essential for Kant as it commands actions be taken according to duty. Kant argues that 'to have moral worth an action must be done from duty'.[60] We focus upon the duty guiding the action and upon the *maxim* (or statement) related to it.[61] This is the heart of Kantian philosophy.

Kant asks whether the proposed act *could* be a universal moral law.[62] Kant tells us that this moral law must be capable of universal conformity as this is the *principle of universalisation*, known as the *categorical imperative*[63] which refers to acts that are 'objectively necessary'.[64] These acts must intend to satisfy morality.[65] Can universal moral laws really apply to all of us all the time?[66] Kant's answer is 'Yes'. Kant acknowledges that every moral decision has the context of specific situations.[67]

The Importance of Moral Duties

While Kant's concern is primarily with *duties* of individuals, these are first tested by universal moral laws to evaluate the wider effects of an act as if it were a settled universal law and whether a person could desire or consent to such a law. Kant gives examples to explain his moral duties.

Duty of Honesty

Kant says if a man borrows money but knows he cannot repay it, he has a dilemma because he realises that unless he promises to repay, he will not

---

58 Ibid.
59 Dierksmeier, above n 54, 606.
60 Kant, above n 2, 19.
61 Ibid., (emphasis added).
62 Ibid., 50–1 (emphasis added).
63 Ibid., 44 (emphasis added).
64 Ibid., 36.
65 Ibid., 37.
66 Dierksmeier, above n 54, 600.
67 Ibid., 601.

receive the loan.[68] Under these circumstances his maxim would be: when in need of money, 'I will borrow' and 'promise to repay it, although I know I shall never do so'.[69] Kant says this maxim is for the borrower's own benefit, but we need to ask two questions: 'Is this right?' and 'What if this maxim became universal law?'.[70] Here Kant examines the consequences of such a moral law. He says that this law could say: 'Anyone who believes himself to be in need could promise what he pleased with the intention of not fulfilling it'.[71] Of course, this 'would make the promise itself' and its purpose, impossible as over time no promisors would be believed.[72] Kant says this law could not be a universal moral law.[73]

It is easy to see why he says this as it is impossible for a universal moral law to support dishonesty. It is simply contradictory that dishonesty could be a universal moral law. Universal dishonesty would undermine trust, which would remove the very meaning of 'promising' in contracts. No rational person would assent to such an outcome.

Duty to help others.

Kant explains that if a 'man, for whom things are going well, sees that others (whom he could help) have to struggle with great hardships' and he thinks "What concern of mine is it?"'.[74] His maxim is: 'There is no requirement to contribute to a person in need, even when it is possible for me to do so'. Kant says that while 'it is possible that a universal law of nature' following this 'maxim could exist, it is nevertheless impossible that such a principle should hold everywhere as a law of nature'.[75]

Kant regards such a universal law as one that would be self-defeating as circumstances could arise where the decision-maker himself could be the one who needs help from others and if this were a universal law, he would be denied assistance.[76] For this reason, the Kantian agent will acknowledge that there needs to be a moral duty to assist the vulnerable in their time of need.

68 Kant above n2, 45.
69 Ibid., 46.
70 Ibid.
71 Ibid.
72 Ibid.
73 Ibid.
74 Ibid.
75 Ibid.
76 Ibid.

Duty of Respect

The duty of respect requires us to always treat others as ends in themselves, not as means to an end.[77] People are valuable in themselves and as human beings they are an end in themselves and this is why people need to be respected and treated with dignity.[78]

Decision-Making Process

Kant acknowledges that we may make decisions for personal convenience from which we formulate a maxim to describe them. We test whether our *subjective* decisions are ethical by rephrasing them in an *objective* sense and applying them *universally*. We then ask what this would mean if this maxim were applied to all as a universal *moral* law. Would this be a rational choice for those interested in promoting ethical decision-making? The answer may be 'No'.

While Kant applies his duties to test the ethicality of a decision, he also tests ethicality by hypothesising the foreseeable consequences. It appears he is engaging in practical wisdom by looking to the personal and commercial reality of the universal moral law. Both Aristotle and Kant appreciate that there is a role for practical wisdom alongside fixed rules. For Aristotle, these rules are the moral and intellectual virtues; for Kant, they are duties, maxims, and universal laws.

Kantian duties are relevant to lawyers' relationships that are informed by legal duties, such as their fiduciary relationship with their clients. Usually, lawyers with their expertise are in a more powerful position vis-á-vis their clients, thus making clients vulnerable to misuse of power by lawyers. Clients are protected by lawyers' fiduciary duty – a legal and ethical duty – to act in the clients' best interests.[79]

Conclusion

This chapter has analysed the core elements of the Aristotelian and Kantian philosophies in enough depth to gain an understanding of them for a particular purpose only, that is, to determine whether their moral content may be used in a new model of TLE and in lawyers' professional obligations. It is a testament to the perceived wisdom of these philosophies that they have

---

77 Dierksmeier, above n 54, 603.
78 De George, above n 3, 65.
79 *Hospital Products Ltd v United States Surgical Corp* (1984) 156 CLR 41.

endured for centuries[80] and their principles remain of interest today to philosophers, academics, and professionals.

In a more general sense, some of the ethical concepts of these philosophies are found in the law: honesty, trust, vulnerability, and duty are elements of the fiduciary obligation at law of all professionals to their clients. The philosophies of Aristotle and Kant have clearly defined ethical principles. They will allow lawyers to apply a philosophical lens to the facts, thus broadening the ethical analysis. Further, ethical reasoning expands the intellectual arguments that lawyers use to justify their actions to themselves and to others.[81] This is a powerful motivation to apply these philosophies to legal ethics. When applied to TLE, they will broaden lawyers' role to include consideration of ethics and permit ethical advice.

Chapter 6 examines the effect of applying Aristotelian and Kantian philosophies to lawyers' key professional obligations. The analysis shows that these moral philosophies will deepen the meaning of existing ethical content within the professional obligations.

---

80 Aristotle's philosophy dates from the third century BC. Kant's philosophy dates from the 18th century.
81 Robert Solomon, *Introducing Philosophy* (Oxford University Press, 8th ed., 2005) 10.

6 Lawyers' Professional Obligations and Moral Philosophies

Chapter 6 shows that the moral philosophies of Aristotle and Kant could increase lawyers' motivation and confidence to meet their professional obligations and thereby enhance this second limb of legal ethics. The chapter studies the main obligations, their importance for the legal profession, and analyses the effect of applying these three philosophies: positivist, Aristotelian, and Kantian. Finally, examples from the James Hardie (JH) case study will illustrate how lawyers could benefit from the philosophies of Aristotle and Kant being applied to their professional obligations.

Each professional obligation has ethical principles within it, further supporting their role in legal ethics. Some of lawyers' professional obligations are legally binding:[1] duties to the law and justice, and fiduciary duties to clients. Other obligations are professionally binding rules, namely: integrity and the practical wisdom and judgement lawyers use when advising clients.

Theoretical legal ethics (TLE) is the first limb of legal ethics. It not only interacts with professional obligations, the second limb of legal ethics, it provides a context for these obligations and the lawyer-to-client relationship by prescribing lawyers' role as one that interprets the law. There is no independent role for ethics. These two limbs of legal ethics have a significant influence over the lawyer-to-client relationship as they dictate a particular role for lawyers and how they practise law.

Lawyers' Professional Integrity

We admire people with integrity[2] in all our relationships, whether these are with professionals, businesspeople, or friends and family. The essence of

---

1 G E Dal Pont, *Lawyers' Professional Responsibility* (Thomson Reuters, 7th ed., 2021) [1.10] 5.
2 Stan van Hooft, *Understanding Virtue Ethics* (Acumen Publishing, 2006) 162.

DOI: 10.4324/9781003264286-6

living with integrity is that we strive to improve our conduct by developing a strong will and intellect.[3] Integrity depends upon a presumption that a person's values are ethical. This reflects the major focus of all moral philosophy: going beyond self-interest to consider the wider perspective of the needs of others and the public benefit.[4] Integrity includes a 'harmonious interaction among the powers of the intellect, will and passions',[5] that requires 'an inner consistency between deed and principle'.[6]

Integrity has a broader meaning for the professions. Acts of integrity are the heart of professional ethics because integrity is what professionals believe in, practice, and live by.[7] Honesty in words and deeds is the essence of professional integrity, it being the personal filter through which all other professional obligations are applied.

The Importance of Integrity for the Legal Profession

We rely upon lawyers' integrity, good character, and trustworthiness because we act upon their advice. Professional integrity for lawyers begins with their admission to legal practice, which requires only 'fit and proper' persons to be admitted. Lawyers are held out to the public as fit to be entrusted 'with their affairs and confidences, as those in whose integrity the public can be confident'.[8] The Supreme Court's admission rules require lawyers to be of good character,[9] this being the basis of integrity in legal practice. Lawyers need to have integrity to retain their practising certificate.

The significance of integrity is recognised in statutes that demand lawyers 'ensure appropriate safeguards are in place for maintaining the integrity of legal services'.[10] Further, lawyers must be 'competent and maintain high ethical and professional standards in the provision of legal services'.[11]

---

3 Michael Macaulay and Surendra Arjoon, 'An Aristotelian-Thomistic Approach to Professional Ethics' (2013) 16(2) *Journal of Markets and Morality* 507, 520.
4 Damian Grace and Stephen Cohen, *Business Ethics* (Oxford University Press, 5th ed., 2013) 6.
5 Macaulay and Arjoon, above n 3, 522.
6 David Luban, 'Integrity: Its Causes and Cures' (2003) 72 *Fordham Law Review* 279, 279.
7 Hugh Breakey, 'Compromise Despite Conviction: Curbing Integrity's Moral Dangers' (2016) 50(3) *Journal of Value Inquiry* 613, 621.
8 *Ex Parte Lenehan* (1948) 77 CLR 403 at 426 per Rich J.
9 *Legal Profession Uniform Law Act 2014* (NSW) s 17(1)(c).
10 Ibid., s 126(a).
11 Ibid., s 3(b).

The spirit of the legislation and its foundation principles tell lawyers to maintain the integrity of the legal profession.[12]

Positivist Philosophy and Integrity

Positivist philosophy makes a limited contribution to integrity. This does not mean positivists want lawyers to act without integrity. It is simply that integrity is not at the forefront of this philosophy. Positivists have other priorities. They see the role of lawyers through a legal, not so much an ethical lens. Positivists claim that the priority in lawyers' role is about the clients and the law, as lawyers 'help clients fit their conduct within the scheme of rights and duties' that the law has created.[13] Some positivists say the role of lawyers is to advance clients' autonomy even if that 'requires excessive and immoral advocacy on behalf of clients',[14] while others say lawyers' role is to secure 'political legitimacy, not justice or ordinary morality'.[15] It is difficult to see how these views advance integrity.

Good character, which also contributes to integrity, may be more difficult to develop under positivist principles. Once lawyers' conduct as guided by positivist TLE is habituated, it may be too late to return[16] or otherwise learn the *moral* goodness required of good character.[17] Ethical advice to clients could constitute lawyers' 'act of integrity',[18] representing honest advice that also protects clients. If such advice could be given under TLE, it would protect lawyers from being in a position where they are asked to help execute 'socially indefensible' but 'technically legal' conduct.[19] For instance, when tobacco company clients demanded their lawyers assist in their denial of the harmful effects of smoking cigarettes.[20] If and when lawyers accede to such requests, it challenges their professional integrity, if at that time there was sufficient evidence to demonstrate there were harmful effects.

---

12 Ibid., s 423(2)(iv) and *Legal Profession Uniform Law Australian Solicitors' Conduct Rules 2015* (NSW) see r 4, 5.

13 W Bradley Wendel, 'Legal Ethics Is About the Law, Not Morality or Justice: A Reply to Critics' (2012) 90(3) *Texas Law Review* 727, 732–3.

14 Tim Dare, 'Mere-Zeal, Hyper-Zeal and the Ethical Obligations of Lawyers' (2004) 7(1) *Legal Ethics* 24, 24.

15 W Bradley Wendel, *Lawyers and Fidelity to Law* (Princeton University Press, 2010, 208.

16 Aristotle, *The Ethics of Aristotle: The Nicomachean Ethics* (J A K Thomson trans., Penguin Books, 1976) 124.

17 Ibid., 116 (emphasis added).

18 Breakey, above n 7, 621.

19 Deborah Rhode, 'Ethics in Practice' in D Rhode (ed.), *Ethics in Practice: Lawyers' Roles Responsibilities and Regulation* (Oxford University Press, 2000) 3, 10.

20 Ibid.

Moreover, a positivist TLE places lawyers in the unenviable position of receiving contradictory messages from their conscience, and from their professional ethics. Their personal ethics, with general concepts of honesty, fairness, and other virtues, contradict or at least rub against the role prescribed for lawyers by a positivist TLE. Our commitment to ethics has to be consistent, in every aspect of our lives, 'including one's professional roles'.[21] Lawyers' professional role, informed by positivist TLE, might direct conduct that would be morally forbidden to a non-lawyer.[22] Lawyers are then likely to experience moral anxiety caused by this 'structural tension' in their role:[23] where inconsistencies arise between their personal and legal ethics. Perversely, a positivist TLE seems to embrace these ethical inconsistencies.

The moral philosophies of Aristotle and Kant have a different approach. They reduce inconsistencies between our personal and professional lives and reinforce our internal harmony. They are thus conducive to the requirements of integrity.

Aristotelian Philosophy and Integrity

Aristotelian philosophy concerns character development by emphasising moral and intellectual virtues.[24] Good character is the basis of integrity.[25] Aristotle's moral virtues of honesty and courage support professional integrity. The virtue of courage would help lawyers to assert their professional independence from their clients enabling them to give advice that is in the best interests of clients. The virtue of honesty would support lawyers giving legal and ethical advice that informs decisions by clients.

Aristotle urges us to choose carefully what we do, as our actions shape our character.[26] Poor choices can be habituated by us almost subconsciously, thus damaging our future integrity and character. We become what the conduct represents.[27] Once habituated, our poor behaviour may be very difficult or impossible to change.[28]

---

21 van Hooft, above n 2, 163.
22 David Luban, 'Misplaced Fidelity' (2012) 90(3) *Texas Law Review* 673, 674.
23 William Simon, *The Practice of Justice: A Theory of Lawyers' Ethics* (Harvard University Press, 1998) 2.
24 Aristotle, above n 16, 90.
25 Sharon Dolovich, 'Ethical Lawyering and the Possibility of Integrity' (2002) 70 *Fordham Law Review* 1629, 1631.
26 Aristotle, above n 16, 123.
27 Ibid.
28 Ibid.

Lawyers too face moral choices, for instance, when they decide whether to accept or refuse clients' requests on professional grounds.[29] Legal practice may have inculcated habits and traits in lawyers that make it hard for them to choose correctly. Lawyers are regularly under pressure from clients to meet their demands because clients want legal advice that promotes their strategies. These may be within the law but simultaneously have unethical consequences for stakeholders, such as employees and creditors.

The moral virtues of honesty and courage clarify lawyers' integrity. Aristotle's intellectual virtues and reasoning also assist lawyers to determine how to develop their professional integrity. In so doing, this further develops lawyers' understanding of integrity and justifies their motivation and confidence to use Aristotelian virtues.

Kantian Philosophy and Integrity

Kant argues that ethical conduct arises from our duties to others:[30] duties to respect others; honesty; and assisting those who are vulnerable.[31] Kantian duties are consistent with moral integrity. A core principle of Kantian ethics is the study of our will and its connection with character. Integrity encourages us to strive to improve our conduct by developing a strong will and intellect.[32] Kant's duty of honesty is a core principle of integrity and of good character and is also an Aristotelian moral virtue. In this way Kantian duties complement[33] Aristotelian moral virtues of good character: honesty, courage, and honour.[34] Kantian duties, therefore, will further contribute to lawyers' integrity. Both philosophies inform and promote integrity from different perspectives.

One would think that lawyers' integrity included giving ethical advice to clients and that this advice would indicate to clients the consequences of using legal advice to make decisions with unethical outcomes for stakeholders. In this way Kantian duties could further develop lawyers' professional obligation of integrity.

29 Justin Oakley and Dean Cocking, *Virtue Ethics and Professional Roles* (Cambridge University Press, 2001) 83.

30 Immanuel Kant, *Foundations of the Metaphysics of Morals* (Lewis White Back trans., Bobbs-Merrill, 1978) 81.

31 Ibid., 19.

32 Macaulay and Arjoon, above n 3, 520.

33 Kant, above n 30, 4–7.

34 Aristotle, above n 16, 104.

Positivist and Moral Philosophies in Re James Hardie: Integrity

The facts of the JH case are reiterated here in summary to give a context for the analysis. Positivist TLE and moral philosophies are applied to this important decision. In February 2001, a board meeting of James Hardie Industries Ltd (JHIL), the parent company, decided to restructure the group. This company had to disclose this to the Australian Securities Exchange (ASX).[35] The company's ASX announcement was approved by this meeting. It included unequivocal statements that JHIL had established a fully funded foundation to provide certainty to asbestos tort victims (both present and future claimants) and that there were sufficient funds to meet future claims.[36]

The reality was that the announcement was 'bereft of substantial truth'.[37] It was alleged that JHIL's managing director knew this.[38] The external lawyers of JHIL, Allens, saw the draft announcement before the February meeting and approved it. Early on the day of the meeting, however, Allens learned that the actuarial data supporting the funding requirements were incomplete,[39] thus putting in doubt the accuracy of the ASX announcement. There was no time before the meeting for Allens to analyse the implications of this.[40] Instead, they relied upon assurances from JHIL's group counsel that funding was adequate, and the statement was not misleading or deceptive. This scenario may raise issues of lawyers' professional integrity. Our three philosophies interpret these facts differently.

Positivists look to lawyers' legal obligations as their 'fundamental ethical obligation'.[41] The legal obligations appear to have been satisfied, especially when given JHIL's assurances, as these were salient for Allens due to the positivist principle of client supremacy. Positivists would say Allens did not breach a positivist TLE, nor professional integrity for that matter.

Aristotelians would question Allens's ready acceptance of its client's assurances. Unlike a positivist TLE's principles of client supremacy that undermines lawyers' independence, Aristotle's principles remove this fetter.

35 *Corporations Act 2001* (Cth) s 674(2).

36 New South Wales, 'Special Commission of Inquiry into the Medical Research and Compensation Foundation' (Report, September 2004) David Jackson, QC, Commissioner ('*Jackson Report*') [22.4] 352 ('Jackson Report') https://www.dpc.nsw.gov.au/publications/categories

37 Ibid., [22.22] 358.

38 Ibid., [22.56] 370.

39 *Australian Securities and Investments Commission v Macdonald (No 11)* [2009] NSWSC 287 [328] 105–6.

40 Ibid., [327] 105.

41 Wendel, above n 15, 89.

The announcement by JHIL was misleading, thus offending the Aristotelian virtue of honesty. Allens, as legal advisers to the board, could have ensured the announcement was amended before being issued or it could have asked JHIL to provide a complete actuarial report to support its announcement. The application of Aristotelian ethics to the new TLE will enable lawyers to identify ethical issues and advise upon them. In this way Aristotelian ethics could inform and give depth to lawyers' professional integrity, as it would have done in this instance.

Kantians would say that Allens failed to respect JHIL by not cautioning it to check the funding figures before contacting the ASX. Kantian ethical duties, including the duty of respect, could clarify professional integrity. If Kantian principles were applied to integrity, they could justify and promote this area of legal ethics.

Lawyers' Duties to the Law and Justice

Justice is 'the quality of being just; righteousness, equitableness, or moral rightness and lawfulness'.[42] Justice is about equality: giving each person his due.[43]

Lawyers' Duties to Law and Justice

Lawyers have a duty to justice.[44] Their professional duties must first and foremost address the proper operation of the legal system and justice. It is in the public interest to do so. The essential ideals of lawyering are to support the law and to achieve justice.[45] Everything in legal practice is shaped by lawyers' duties to the law and justice.[46]

When the Supreme Court admits lawyers to the roll of legal practitioners, they promise to uphold the law.[47] They become officers of the Court[48] with a 'paramount duty to it and to the administration of justice'.[49] Lawyers

---

42 Arthur Delbridge et al. (eds), *The Macquarie Dictionary* (Macquarie Library, 1982) 961.

43 Richard De George, *Business Ethics* (Prentice Hall, 7th ed., 2010) 76.

44 *Legal Profession Uniform Law Australian Solicitors' Conduct Rules 2015* (NSW) r 3; *Legal Profession Uniform Law Act 2014* (NSW) s 423(2)(a).

45 Oakley and Cocking, above n 29, 75.

46 Christine Parker and Adrian Evans, *Inside Lawyers' Ethics* (Cambridge University Press, 3rd ed., 2018) 306.

47 David Wilkins, 'In Defense of Law *and* Morality: Why Lawyers Should have a Prima Facie Duty to Obey the Law' (1996) 38 *William and Mary Law Review* 269, 290.

48 *Legal Profession Uniform Law Act 2014* (NSW) s 25.

49 *Legal Profession Uniform Law Australian Solicitors' Conduct Rules 2015* (NSW) r 3; *Legal Profession Uniform Law Act 2014* (NSW) s 423(2)(a).

participate 'in the legal system' in their role of officers of the Court, and as such they must respect the law and how it is administered.[50] This is 'an overriding duty'[51] and the raison d'être of the legal profession. Justice does not reside in clients' interests alone.[52] The choice is clear. Lawyers must first uphold their duty to the court and to justice.

Lawyers' duty to the court requires them to be independent from their clients to enable them to make the 'independent judgment'[53] necessary to fulfil their professional duty. *Rondel v Worsley*[54] distinguishes lawyers' duty to clients to raise all issues that will advance clients' cases, from lawyers' duty to the court and the administration of justice as this includes a duty 'to the standards of [the] profession, and to the public'.[55] The idea that the law applies equally to all is at its core. This is the fairness embraced by justice. It explains the interconnectedness of law and justice.

Positivist Philosophy: Law and Justice

Positivists regard the law objectively[56] without reaching a conclusion upon the law's 'justness or merit'.[57] Lawyers are directed to advance clients' interests without considering 'the moral worthiness' or 'justness of their causes'.[58] The effect of this is that lawyers may assist clients to execute socially questionable, but nevertheless legal, decisions.[59] This places lawyers in a position where their professional obligations to the law and justice appear to be diluted by positivist principles. This could have dire consequences for lawyers. If they think their main role is to interpret the law, this is all they will do. Creative lawyering: massaging 'rules, distinctions, meanings and facts to serve their clients' purposes',[60] could become their mode of practice. In clear cases of anticipated injustice, clients' interests should *not* prevail.

---

50 Dal Pont, above n 1, [19.05] 653.
51 Parker and Evans, above n 46, 178.
52 Dolovich, above n 25, 1630.
53 Dal Pont, above n 1, [17.10] 571.
54 [1969] 1 AC 191.
55 Ibid., 227.
56 Augusto Zimmermann, *Western Legal Theory: History, Concepts and Perspectives* (LexisNexis Butterworths, 2013) 66.
57 Ibid., 82.
58 Allan Hutchinson, *Fighting Fair: Legal Ethics for an Adversarial Age* (Cambridge University Press, 2015) 19.
59 Rhode, above n 19, 10.
60 Hutchinson, above n 58, 19.

Clients' loyalty is envisaged by the positivist philosophy's *Partisanship Principle*. However, this 'has never been an absolute obligation of lawyers' per se.[61] This is because loyalty to clients could place lawyers 'at odds with justice' and perhaps even have them working 'against the law'.[62] In addition, the principle of clients' loyalty raises questions as to whether a positivist philosophy renders lawyers 'a mere instrument of the clients' interests',[63]service providers, and quasi-professionals. Such a change in the lawyer-to-client relationship subjects lawyers 'to moral risk',[64] potentially being unable to realise the ideal of justice.[65]

> [I]f the client's aims are unjust the lawyer becomes an accomplice in injustice – not just a bystander, but an active agent of injustice, using skills of thought and speech (the "moral faculties") to effectuate injustice.[66]

Aristotelian Philosophy: Law and Justice

Aristotle relates justice to character and implies that persons of good character value justice.[67] These persons uphold the moral virtues of honesty, courage, and compassion.[68] These virtues are needed to satisfy the principles of justice: moral rightness and fairness. Aristotle regards justice as part of legal compliance as a just person obeys the law and is fair.[69]

Aristotle distinguishes between justice in the conduct of one's own affairs as being a limited justice, whereas when justice is exercised in relation to other people, this constitutes the deeper meaning of justice.[70] Aristotle argues that 'justice is that state in virtue' where 'a just man' [or woman] is 'capable of doing just acts from choice'.[71] Justice and fairness for individuals and the community inform Aristotle's overarching principles of character development. Aristotelian principles clarify the meaning

---

61 Nancy Moore, 'In the Interests of Justice: Balancing Client Loyalty and the Public Good in the Twenty-First Century' (2002) 70 *Fordham Law Review* 1775, 1777.
62 David Luban, *Lawyers and Justice: An Ethical Study,* (Princeton University Press, 1988) 12.
63 Ibid., 13.
64 David Luban, 'Smith Against the Ethicists' (1990) 9(4) *Law and Philosophy* 417, 428.
65 Ibid.
66 Ibid.
67 Aristotle, above n 16, 171
68 Ibid.
69 Ibid., 104.
70 Ibid., 174.
71 Ibid., 186.

of the law and justice and in doing so advance these important professional obligations.

Kantian Philosophy: Law and Justice

Kantian moral principles in legal ethics offer additional support for lawyers' duties. Lawyers are required to 'balance the public good against the demands of' clients.[72] This is about benefitting others, beyond self and the clients. Kantian duties to others would assist lawyers to fulfil the goals of justice. The duties of honesty, respect, and protection of vulnerable persons,[73] advance the cause of justice. One would think that justice could not be achieved if legal practice permitted dishonesty. Respect is essential to justice, as encouraging clients to respect stakeholders could produce decisions that were fair and honourable. Protecting vulnerable persons (such as stakeholders) could also serve justice and is another reason for clients to pursue decisions that are fair.

Justice also concerns equality. Kant's universal moral laws from which Kantian duties are developed, embrace equality too. Further, equality is only meaningful if Kant's ethical duty of respect is upheld in the sense that all people deserve to be equally respected without discrimination. Kant's ethical duties of honesty and protection of the vulnerable also relate to justice, as do the principles of moral rightness. These principles coincide with the need to protect the vulnerable from dishonest or misleading conduct and abuses of power. In this way, Kantian duties contribute to the goal of justice.

The value of Kant's ethical duties is they give lawyers a broader perspective and greater clarity of the ideals of justice and the law. Kantian duties are likely to reinforce these ideals, thereby strengthening lawyers' duties and the moral core within them.

Positivist and Moral Philosophies in Re James Hardie: Law and Justice

We saw in the case study what happened to the tort victims when compensation funding provisions were inadequate. This could reasonably be called unjust. By July 2002, when updated actuarial reports were available, the Medical Research and Compensation Foundation (MRCF) revealed that its

---

72 Eliot Freidson, *Professionalism: The Third Logic* (University of Chicago Press, 2001) 222.
73 Kant, above n 30, 19.

funds would be depleted within five years[74] with '80% of future victims being unlikely to have their claims considered, let alone met'.[75]

The parent company, JHIL, had received substantial financial benefit from the operations of the employer subsidiaries: A\$2.4 billion, before tax, between 1969 and 1997.[76] However, JHIL was prepared, and legally able to, distance itself from financial responsibility. Under positivist TLE principles of client supremacy, lawyers are hesitant to challenge their clients. Allens did seek and receive assurances from JHIL on the matter of funding. However, if Allens had had recourse to Aristotelian and Kantian philosophies, it could have assessed the wider needs of justice.[77]

The value of Aristotle's virtues is that they directly address the essence of justice and fairness and thus can more readily serve the concept of justice. A just outcome in the JH case would have resulted in JHIL taking more responsibility for providing adequate funds to tort victims. It is argued that Aristotelian moral virtues of justice, fairness, and equity as part of the new moral TLE, increase the likelihood of a just outcome.

Kantian duties and universal moral principles would also have influenced Allens to focus upon their professional obligation to justice rather than client demands as required by a positivist TLE. Kantian duties of respect for others and assistance for vulnerable people would have achieved a fair outcome as Allens could then have identified the justice issue in JHIL's instructions.

Lawyers and Clients: Fiduciary and Confidentiality Duties

A fiduciary duty is one that originated in equity at general law and under statute.[78] It is also an *ethical* principle.[79] The duty relates to lawyers, usually in positions of power, with clients being the vulnerable party in the relationship.[80] It is why under this duty, lawyers have to act in the best interests of their clients. The confidentiality duty is one that lawyers

---

74 *Jackson Report,* above n 36, [26.75] 483.

75 Ibid., [27.22] 496.

76 Ibid., [30.14], 555.

77 Dolovich, above n 25, 1630.

78 *Legal Profession Uniform Law Act 2014* (NSW) s 423(2)(b) and *Legal Profession Uniform Law Australian Solicitors' Conduct Rules 2015* (NSW) r 4.1.1.

79 Paul D Finn, 'The Fiduciary Principle' in Timothy G Youdan (ed.), *Equity, Fiduciaries and Trusts* (Carswell, Toronto, 1989) 55 (emphasis added).

80 *Hospital Products Ltd v United States Surgical Corp* (1984) 156 CLR 41.

owe to clients not to disclose clients' confidences.[81] Trust is the ethical substance in both duties.

Lawyers' Fiduciary and Confidentiality Duties

There may be tension between lawyers and clients when lawyers are determining clients' best interests. Clients often want the fiduciary duty to have a narrow focus upon themselves and their interests. A literal interpretation of the fiduciary duty could weaken lawyers' professionalism. Lawyers are not expected to prioritise this duty if to do so would compromise their professional integrity. Further, acting in the clients' best interests as fiduciaries must not be contrary to the interests of justice.

The term, clients' *interests,* is widely interpreted. Commercial interests are often clients' priority and lawyers must take account of them. Legal and equitable interests inform clients' rights and obligations, and these too are considered by lawyers. One would think it in the best interests of clients to advise them of ethical issues arising from the use of legal advice where it could affect clients' ongoing relationships with stakeholders such as creditors, employees, and customers.

The confidentiality duty owed to clients does not override lawyers' duty to the court and the administration of justice. For example, lawyers have a duty to the court to disclose information relevant to court proceedings. Another limitation upon the duty of confidentiality is that 'keeping information confidential is not an end in itself' as to do so may not be in the public good.[82]

Positivist Philosophy: Fiduciary and Confidentiality Duties

Acting in the clients' best interests and keeping clients' confidences, fit well within a positivist philosophy as both put clients at the centre of lawyers' concerns. However, positivist TLE and its *partisanship principle* of client loyalty 'lacks ethical content'.[83] Consequently, lawyers tend to see ethics as being less relevant, thus potentially restricting the scope of their professional duties, including the fiduciary duty.[84] It could well be in the clients' best interests for lawyers to advise that their strategy is unethical, and it

---

81 *Legal Profession Uniform Law Act 2014* (NSW) s 423(2)(b)(i).

82 Moore, above n 61, 1779.

83 Ysaiah Ross, *Ethics in Law: Lawyers' Responsibility and Accountability in Australia* (LexisNexis Butterworths, 5th ed., 2010) 45.

84 Paul D Finn, *Fiduciary Obligations* (Law Book Company, 1977).

needs amendment. Lawyers as fiduciaries and professionals, cannot ignore the morality of clients' causes as these may affect the reputations of both clients and lawyers, yet positivist TLE's *neutrality principle* requires lawyers to do just that.

Many believe that the 2008 global financial crisis was caused by ethical failures in business.[85] Others think that there was a failure by professionals as gatekeepers, for example the role of credit rating agencies who verified and certified inferior banking products.[86] Corporate lawyers, as legal advisers to the banks at this time, would have encountered ethical issues, but a positivist TLE prevented them from giving ethical advice. Paradoxically, this lack of ethical advice in relation to clients' practices may have led lawyers to fail in their legal duty as fiduciaries to protect clients' best interests.

Aristotelian Philosophy: Fiduciary and Confidentiality Duties

Aristotelian philosophy includes the altruistic purpose of beneficence. Ethics is a necessary component of the fiduciary duty, and it is legitimate, therefore, to regard ethics as a matter that *is* in the best interests of clients. Aristotle's moral virtue of courage could enrich lawyers' fiduciary duty. If this virtue is applied to the fiduciary duty, it would permit lawyers to independently assess clients' best interests and communicate this. Clients need, although they may not want, an objective professional opinion from their lawyers. Aristotelian moral virtues would enable lawyers to better fulfil their fiduciary duty by giving clients a more complete picture of what is in their best interests. Lawyers too benefit, as the professional independence that they need to properly determine what is in clients' best interests will not be compromised.

The duty of confidentiality is also framed by ethics because betrayal of a confidence is a breach of the moral virtue of trustworthiness. Still, there may be strong ethical (and legal) reasons for lawyers to apply the moral virtue of honesty and disclose to others. For example, public interest may dictate clients' matters that raise community health and/or related environmental concerns must be disclosed, usually to a regulatory body.[87] This type of situation creates an inverse relationship with the duty of confidentiality:

85 Victor Lewis et al, 'Was the 2008 Financial Crisis Caused by a Lack of Corporate Ethics?' (2010) 4(2) *Global Journal of Business Research* 77, 77.
86 John Coffee Jr, 'What went wrong? An Initial Inquiry into the Causes of the 2008 Financial Crisis' (2009) 9(1) *Journal of Corporate Law Studies* 1, 1.
87 Dal Pont, above n 1, [10.75] 362–3.

the stronger the ethical reasons to disclose, the weaker is the duty of con-fidentiality.[88] If lawyers are knowledgeable in ethics, they will be able to identify ethical issues in their fiduciary and confidentiality duties which will alert them to consequential legal issues. This protects both lawyers and their clients. Moral virtues will also assist lawyers in exercising their confidentiality duty, directing them to consider ethical issues. Legal concerns may arise from some of these issues.

Kantian Philosophy: Fiduciary and Confidentiality Duties

Kantian moral duties to vulnerable persons, honesty, and respect are relevant to the fiduciary duty. Lawyers could include in their advice consideration of the stakeholders who might be affected by clients' decisions. For example, in the case study, Allens gave advice on the group's restructure. This was lawful advice that assisted JHIL to real-ise its commercial goals, yet the impact upon stakeholders was not suf-ficiently considered. If Kantian principles had been part of TLE they would have permitted Allens to advise JHIL that it could be in breach of its ethical duties to assist vulnerable tort victims. Instead, as positivist TLE includes neither stakeholders nor ethics, this was not considered. Inadequate funding provisions for tort victims were the consequence. This, in time, proved to be damaging to JHIL and ultimately led to the New South Wales Government initiating an inquiry into JHIL's fund-ing arrangements.[89] If Allens had been able to consider Kantian duties these would have broadened the fiduciary duty and their advice to JHIL. Instead, JHIL's executives were required to spend months testifying before the Commission of Inquiry to explain their decisions.

Including Kantian principles to inform lawyers' advice is justified. This clarifies for clients what is in their best interests and assists lawyers to truly act in their clients' best interests. When clients act unethically and then claim their actions resulted from lawyers' advice, it is difficult for the public not to feel some disquiet towards lawyers too.

Lawyers' Practical Wisdom and Judgement

Lawyers' duties to the law and justice; and their fiduciary and confidential-ity duties are legally binding. Lawyers' integrity and their practical wisdom and judgement are professionally binding rules.

---

88 Luban, above n 62, 202.
89 *Jackson Report*, above n 36, 1.

Lawyers and Practical Wisdom

Practical wisdom relates to judgement: the heart of good advice. The role of practical wisdom involves the final analytical step that precedes lawyers' advice to clients. It is about deliberating upon 'both the ends and the means of practical conduct'[90] Practical wisdom is 'the ability to reason and intuit one's way to a conclusion based upon a combination of experience, virtues, values, and knowledge (exercising a combination of both rational and emotional intelligence)'.[91] It also includes the circumstances of clients, and the practical context in which lawyers' advice will be applied.

Positivist Philosophy and Practical Wisdom

A positivist philosophy tells lawyers that client interests take priority and are best served by ignoring ordinary morality,[92] thereby potentially removing the ethical component of practical wisdom. This restricts the value of lawyers' practical wisdom. If the lawyers' perspective is narrowed in this way, then practical wisdom could become client-centred only. This may be insufficient as it encourages advice where justice and ethics are diminished, and this is contrary to the best interests of the clients and the profession.

Aristotelian Philosophy and Practical Wisdom

Aristotelian philosophy has most to offer practical wisdom. Aristotle's practical wisdom involves 'appreciating one's situation and knowing how to act accordingly'; as well as 'judgement, the ability to determine' … 'what is right and proper'.[93] Aristotle's moral and intellectual virtues could guide lawyers in the exercise of practical wisdom. Aristotle is not concerned with mere thought, but rather 'purposive and practical thought'.[94] Practical wisdom or prudence is the *objective* standard of the prudent man.[95] Prudence is the vital link between the intellectual and moral virtues. Both virtues inform integrity and practical wisdom.[96]

---

90   James Murphy, 'Practical Reason and Moral Psychology in Aristotle and Kant' (2001) 18(2) *Social Philosophy and Policy Foundation* 257, 259–60.
91   Stephen Pepper, 'Three Dichotomies in Lawyers' Ethics: (With Particular Attention to the Corporation as Client)' (2015) 28 *The Georgetown Journal of Legal Ethics* 1069, 1103.
92   Wendel, above n 15, 85.
93   James O Urmson, *Aristotle's Ethics* (Blackwell Publishers, 1988) 81–2.
94   Aristotle, above n 16, 205.
95   Ibid., 224.
96   Ibid., 222.

Lawyers ought to think for and with their clients in relation to clients' objectives and whether these are wise, rather than simply advising them only upon the legal way to realise objectives.[97] This is 'deliberative judgement' and for this lawyers need 'practical wisdom' that is only possible if they 'possess certain traits of character' that are important to practical wisdom.[98] Aristotle examines the type of character that we require to make good choices in deliberation.[99] He argues that our choices imply the involvement of 'a rational principle and thought'.[100] Aristotle wants us to take *action* to realise a practical cause.[101] The complete performance of the functioning of man is based upon combining '*prudence* and *moral virtue*' where 'virtue ensures the correctness of the *end* at which we aim, and prudence the *means* towards it.'[102]

Pepper questions the 'basis for the ethical choices' that lawyers ought to make in their legal practice and he recommends that a better basis of ethical choice for lawyers in exercising practical wisdom might be found in their good character.[103] Lawyers of good character 'exercising educated ethical deliberation would be better able to deal with the complexity of human interaction and the multiplicity of relevant factors far more flexibly and effectively'.[104]This supports the view that practical wisdom, when informed by Aristotelian virtues, would be a worthwhile guide. Lawyers could easily identify with these as their goals in professional practice. Their expertise as an intellectual virtue, without ethics, is one-dimensional. It is argued that Aristotelian philosophy makes a substantial contribution to lawyers' practical wisdom by also giving lawyers moral virtues to consider when they exercise practical wisdom in their advice to clients.

Kantian Philosophy and Practical Wisdom

Kant critically examines practical reason.[105] He delineates a role for the practical aspects of decisions. The significance of this role to his core philosophy is that the practical use of reason concerns Kant's categorical

---

97 Anthony Kronman, *The Lost Lawyer: Failing Ideals of the Legal Profession* (Belknap Press of Harvard University Press, 1993) 133.
98 Ibid., 134.
99 Urmson, above n 93, 22.
100 Aristotle, above n 16, 117–18.
101 Ibid., 213.
102 Ibid., 222 (emphasis added).
103 Pepper, above n 91, 1104.
104 Ibid., 1103–4.
105 Kant, above n 30, 73.

imperative: whether a decision *could* be a universal moral law. Kant says practical reason is needed for conduct whose origin is in moral law,[106] from which Kantian duties originate. Kantian philosophy adds another perspective to practical wisdom because universality is a method of testing the practicality of a decision. In this way, we could say that Kantian philosophy clarifies the meaning of practical wisdom.

Positivist and Moral Philosophies in Re James Hardie: Practical Wisdom

The present process of practical wisdom for lawyers begins with formulating clients' legal advice. A major part of Allens's advice to JHIL concerned a proposed restructure of the JH group. This required complex legal advice ranging across corporate, taxation, and property law. There were also ongoing matters concerning employees' claims for compensation under tort law. This advice relied upon the considerable expertise of Allens. Lawyers then must comply with their professional obligations and practical wisdom. Positivist TLE influences these steps.

Allens had to use practical wisdom to determine how best JHIL might practically achieve its goal of protecting the group from financial liability while meeting its other goal of providing sufficient funds in MRCF for tort victims. The legal advice achieved the goal to protect the group but failed in the funding goal. It is not known if Allens was aware, or suspicious, of JHIL's actual funding position at the time it gave advice.

Allens could have cautioned JHIL that there were unresolved issues with tort victim compensation and that this end goal to protect tort victims may not be realised. Once the public, investors, and tort victims and their families discovered that JHIL had protected itself at the expense of proper protection for tort victims, the public demanded an explanation from JHIL. Later it was revealed that JHIL decided to cancel the partly paid shares, a necessary protection for tort victims.

The JH case provides examples for Aristotelian and Kantian philosophies to be applied to practical wisdom. Aristotelian virtues refer to clients' goals as well as the means to achieve them. When moral virtues are applied to these goals to protect tort victims, the advice given breaches these virtues. The stakeholder tort victims were not financially protected as actuarial data were incomplete and available funds to compensate future victims were inadequate.

---

106 Ibid., 34.

Kant's universal moral laws were also breached as it would not be morally acceptable to have a Kantian maxim that said: when in need of court approval for a restructure, we will give an assurance that we have a plan to protect stakeholders but after approval, we will significantly amend the plan. If this maxim became a universal moral law, it would make business assurances to courts worthless. This could not be a universal moral law. Allens could, therefore, have advised JHIL that their intention to cancel the partly paid shares was neither practical nor ethical. Again, the difficulty is that Allens probably was unaware of JHIL's intention, although it knew it was legally possible to cancel these shares. If Allens had suspected JHIL's intention to cancel, or was aware of that legal possibility, then practical wisdom would have required Allens to advise against cancellation.

Conclusion

Aristotelian and Kantian philosophies applied to lawyers' professional obligations and rules will broaden and enhance them. We can observe the advantage gained by lawyers in practical wisdom which is relevant to lawyers' advice throughout the lawyer-to-client relationship. The guidance provided by these moral philosophies would help lawyers to make more informed judgements in relation to clients' goals and the practical means available to clients to achieve them. Aristotelian and Kantian moral principles are complementary and the contribution of each further develops existing ethics within lawyers' professional obligations.

Chapter 7 explains and analyses the structure of the new moral model of TLE and its contribution to lawyers' professional obligations. It centres upon a reasoning process for lawyers to make ethical decisions when formulating their legal and ethical advice, by including Aristotelian and Kantian moral philosophies. It also considers legal practice issues and offers guidance to lawyers when communicating their advice to clients so that they do so in a manner that is meaningful to clients.

7 A New Model of Legal Ethics

The first limb of legal ethics, positivist theoretical legal ethics (TLE), provides a template for legal practice. It influences the second limb, lawyers' professional obligations. Previous chapters have shown that positivist TLE has created problems for lawyers in both parts of legal ethics.

The purpose of Chapter 7 is to present a new *moral* model of TLE that applies the moral philosophies of Aristotle and Kant to address these problems. This is a significant reform of legal ethics as it adds a moral role to lawyers' primary role of giving only legal advice. The new model of TLE has three core principles and three steps, both summarised below.

Step I in this new model shows the importance for lawyers of developing moral sensitivity to identify ethical issues in client instructions. Step II elaborates and guides lawyers in the development of moral reasoning by drawing upon their moral integrity. Practical wisdom is also required in the reasoning process when lawyers assess how clients will implement their advice. Steps I and II are applied to the decisions of James Hardie's lawyers, Allens. The hypothesis is that a new moral TLE would have better supported Allens's professionalism and led to more ethical decisions by its clients. Step III is lawyers' dialogue with clients to explain their advice.

Core Principles of a Moral TLE

Primary Obligation of Professional Integrity

This principle requires lawyers to advance the interests of clients within the bounds of law and morality. This acknowledges lawyers' fiduciary duty to act in the best interests of clients. The limitations that apply in a positivist TLE that make clients' interests paramount, do not apply under the new model which requires lawyers to view clients' interests independently through the lens of lawyers' legal and professional duties and integrity.

DOI: 10.4324/9781003264286-7

Principle of Morality

Here, lawyers should specifically consider the morality of the actions that clients require lawyers to undertake to advance the clients' cause, or that of a third party. This principle also directs lawyers to consider the morality of their own actions to satisfy clients or third-party strategies and whether these actions are ethical.

Principle of Accountability

If lawyers adhere to the above two principles, neither third-party observers nor the lawyers should regard themselves as wrongdoers, in legal or moral terms.[1] Lawyers, however, are accountable professionally if they fail to uphold principles one and two.

Steps in a Moral TLE (summary)

Step I: Moral Sensitivity

- Lawyers' moral sensitivity is developed by moral awareness of ethical issues in clients' instructions. This alerts lawyers that clients may be deliberately or inadvertently about to engage in unethical conduct. Aristotle supports good character by developing the moral virtues: fairness, compassion, honesty, and justice. These virtues increase moral sensitivity and aid lawyers' integrity.

Step II: Moral Reasoning and Practical Wisdom

- Moral reasoning is more specific to the deeper ethical thinking we need to evaluate issues identified in Step I. These issues also relate to practical wisdom where lawyers assess how clients will implement their advice. Moral reasoning coexists with legal reasoning. This is the basis of lawyers' legal and ethical advice to clients: expertise, integrity, reasoning, practical wisdom, reflection, and judgement.
- Aristotle's intellectual virtues of competence and excellence apply as do the moral virtues used in Step I: Moral Sensitivity. Kant's moral reasoning concerns the duties of honesty, respect, and protecting the vulnerable. The practicalities of a decision are determined by whether it could be a universal moral law.

---

1 Barbara Mescher 'Corporate Law Practice: Legal Advice and Ethics' (2018) 92 *Australian Law Journal* 636, 649.

Step III: Dialogue with Clients

- Lawyers explain their legal and ethical advice to clients. They persuade clients to accept their advice by appealing to clients' best interests and showing them that Aristotle's virtues and Kant's duties support those interests.
- Moral imagination may be used by lawyers to assist clients to realise their goals by making decisions that are both ethical and legal. This could mean that clients will need to amend strategies. They may refuse to do so. This is when lawyers' professional independence becomes more important, especially if their higher responsibility to the law, justice, the profession, and the public good are at stake.

Cognitive Processes and Legal Practice

Knowledge of behavioural science will enable lawyers to adopt preventive measures to protect and enact their ethicality. The broad cognitive errors most pertinent to legal practice and ethical issues include delusions of our ethicality and diminution of our cognitive capacity. These are relevant to lawyers' initial and continuing assessments of their clients' instructions and the lawyers' perception of ethical and legal issues. It is important that lawyers understand cognitive deficits: what they are; how to address them; and how they may undermine professional obligations and the quality of advice.

The Delusion of Our Own Ethicality

Research has revealed that human beings deceive themselves regarding their own ethicality.[2] We have 'ethical blind spots' caused by the 'gap between how ethical we think we are and how ethical we truly are'.[3] Under this delusion we are likely to behave how we want to behave rather than our own prediction 'that we will behave as we think we *should* behave'.[4]

When lawyers inform their clients of their advice, it would be beneficial for these lawyers to know how the delusion of ethicality may affect their own and their clients' decision-making. Lawyers will then be able to use behavioural ethics to advise clients. Maybe the decisions clients had thought were ethical could be subject to a delusion. Further, the benefit to lawyers of being informed by moral principles in the new TLE, is that they

2 Max H Bazerman and Ann E Tenbrunsel, *Blind Spots: Why We Fail to do What's Right and What to do About It* (Princeton University Press, 2011).

3 Ibid., 1.

4 Ibid., 153.

could advise clients of the relationship between the lawyers' legal advice and possible ethical outcomes from decisions clients may make using that advice.

The misconception of our own ethicality relates to our two systems of thinking. System one, which is our less considered automatic thinking, contributes to the delusion and is more likely to be unethical.[5] System two, reflective and reasoned thinking, is more suitable for complex decisions.[6] If we are aware of the delusion of our ethicality we can address this by consciously engaging in system two thinking to take us 'toward the ideal image we hold of ourselves'.[7] This is essential for lawyers to avoid the delusion's negative effects: the weakening of their obligation to act with professional integrity. This professional rule is now a legal obligation: 'ensuring lawyers are competent and maintain high ethical and professional standards in the provision of legal services'.[8]

If lawyers believe themselves to be more ethical than they are, the consequences are twofold. Firstly, they may feel there is no need to make the greater effort required in system two thinking. Secondly, they may fail to sufficiently evaluate the ethicality of their own decisions and the decisions of clients. Moreover, the ethicality delusion could create a reluctance on the part of lawyers to adopt the new moral model of legal ethics if they believe they do not need it.

Factors in Diminished Cognitive Capacity

When clients ask lawyers to give them professional advice, the matters are usually factually and legally diverse and their resolution subject to deadlines. Individual lawyers may be involved simultaneously with advice work in relation to multiple case files. Corporate lawyers have the added complexity of dealing with legal abstractions that include the company form and financial interests. Lawyers need to be aware of ethical misconceptions and the factors that interact with our cognitive processes to produce negative effects for lawyers' behaviour. Some of these may lead to unethical decisions. Four related factors occur in legal practice where there is an extensive caseload. Each one impacts upon the other and their cumulative effect is to further diminish cognitive capacity.

---

5 Ibid., 153–4.
6 Ibid.
7 Ibid., 154.
8 *Legal Profession Uniform Law Act 2014* (NSW) s 3(b).

The first factor is the stress of handling such a large volume of work. When humans experience stress, their cognitive capacity is diminished.[9] Within less than a minute stress can change our thinking, how we come to our decisions, our conduct, and how other people are able to influence us.[10] Another effect is that stress skews our thinking to a more pessimistic view where we tend to 'focus on what can go wrong'.[11] This pessimism may mean lawyers promote a different legal strategy, one that may not be the clients' best option. Awareness of, rather than a concentration upon, negative factors, will lead to a more balanced view by lawyers.

Reduced caseloads are a work practice issue. Reduced stress and burnout in the profession could provide substantial health benefits for lawyers. Researchers have found that stress and mental health 'are a serious concern for the legal profession in Australia'.[12] A smaller lawyer caseload benefits clients too as it helps limit lawyers' cognitive shortcuts in decision-making and is likely to produce a higher standard of advice.

The second factor, linked to the first, is the time pressure of deadlines that are a common feature of legal practice, due to the nature of the legal process and clients' demands. Busy people are less likely to have the time they may need to reflect under system two thinking. Therefore, they are more likely to participate in system one thinking that is quick but can produce unethical decisions.[13]

The third factor relates to the volume and complexity of decisions that lawyers are required to make throughout their day. It would be impossible to accomplish this without some 'preconscious filters and shortcuts'.[14] However, lawyers' advice could be less effective if relevant facts and ethical concerns are not adequately considered.

The fourth factor is that lawyers' cognitive capacity is diminished by something more subtle and, therefore, less likely to be noticed. When lawyers enter a relationship with clients they agree to advise and represent them. This is a commitment to both their clients and to themselves. If, subsequently, lawyers encounter information that shows there may be 'harmful consequences flowing from that commitment', research suggests we tend

9   Donald Langevoort, 'Where Were the Lawyers? A Behavioral Inquiry into Lawyers' Responsibility for Clients' Fraud' (1993) 48 *Vanderbilt Law Review* 75, 78.

10 Tali Sharot, *The Influential Mind: What the Brain Reveals about our Power to Change Others* (Little, Brown, 2017) 133.

11 Ibid., 136.

12 Janet Chan, Suzanne Poynton and Jasmin Bruce, 'Lawyering Stress and Work Culture: An Australian Study' (2014) 37(3) *University of New South Wales Law Journal* 1062, 1062.

13 Bazerman and Tenbrunsel, above n 2, 164.

14 Langevoort, above n 9, 99.

to suppress that information.[15] We perceive this as a threat to our self-belief that we are good people.[16] This is a serious negative effect. Just when lawyers should be interpreting this information as something requiring further attention, they are likely to suppress it, leading to a reduction of their cognitive vigilance.[17] Lawyers need to retain this to objectively assess the client and relevant information and to avoid being unwittingly complicit in their clients' legal and ethical misconduct, such as financial fraud.[18]

The new moral TLE does not have an emphasis wholly upon clients (unlike a positivist model). Rather, the new model permits lawyers to view their clients at arms' length before making a commitment to represent them. This means that when, or if, lawyers encounter subsequent adverse information, they are less likely to subconsciously suppress it. After all, some clients do lie to their lawyers.[19] In order to detect this, lawyers need to continuously, and objectively, appraise clients and their instructions.

The contribution of psychologists in relation to our cognitive processes and moral development is valuable for lawyers. It informs them of factors that could influence their decisions. The existence of cognitive delusions and diminished cognitive capacities are not necessarily barriers to ethical decision-making. Instead, we lessen their negative effects by being aware of their existence and consciously engaging in system two thinking and its heightened state of reasoning.

Step I: Moral Sensitivity

Moral sensitivity[20] involves a 'capacity to recognize that a situation has moral dimensions'.[21] Lawyers exercise their moral sensitivity under the new model by scrutinising client instructions and goals and applying Aristotelian and Kantian ethics. This has the effect of informing lawyers of the possibility of clients engaging in unethical conduct. Lawyers are now on notice that this is the environment in which their advice will be formulated.

---

15 Ibid., 102–3.
16 Ibid., 103.
17 Ibid., 102.
18 Ibid., 95.
19 Ibid.
20 Hugh Breakey, 'Building Ethics Regimes: Capabilities, Obstacles and Supports for Professional Ethical Decision-Making' (2017) Vol 40(1) *University of New South Wales Law Journal* 322, 329.
21 Allan Hutchinson, *Fighting Fair: Legal Ethics for an Adversarial Age* (Cambridge University Press, 2015) 9.

They will also be aware that their conduct of clients' matters must be more finely attuned to lawyers' professional obligations.

Enhancing Moral Sensitivity

When we apply Aristotelian principles, they raise our moral sensitivity. We are then able to consider the facts through the filter of the moral virtues. Aristotle says if we develop our character, we are more likely to make ethical decisions.[22] The process begins by adopting moral virtues, and these incorporate a standard of excellence.[23] The virtues include fairness, compassion, honesty, courage, and justice.[24] Aristotle shows our choices are important.[25] What we choose to do, more than the actions themselves, determines character.[26] Habituation of good choices is essential.

Kant also has much to offer the development of moral sensitivity. Important Kantian duties are to assist vulnerable persons,[27] to be honest,[28] to respect persons,[29] and to treat others 'as an end' (in themselves) 'never as a means only'.[30]

Lawyers and Moral Sensitivity

The nature of legal practice, especially corporate law practice, suggests that clients require both ethical and legal advice. If clients' goals involve facilitation by lawyers using legal means to unjustly or unfairly defeat the rights of others, such as stakeholders, this is an ethical issue for both lawyers and their clients. Some clients may use lawyers' legal advice to progress the clients' unethical and unlawful conduct.[31] Lawyers have a role to act in the

---

22 Aristotle, *The Ethics of Aristotle: The Nicomachean Ethics* (Penguin Books, 1976, translated by JAK Thomson) 90.

23 Aristotle, *Nicomachean Ethics* (Focus Publishing/R Pullins, 350BC/2002, translated by Joe Sachs) 5.

24 Aristotle, above n 22, 104.

25 Ibid., 116.

26 Ibid.

27 Immanuel Kant, *Foundations of the Metaphysics of Morals* (Bobbs-Merrill Educational Publishing, 1978, translated by Lewis White Beck) 47.

28 Ibid., 45.

29 Ibid., 53.

30 Ibid., 54.

31 David Kershaw and Richard Moorhead, 'Consequential Responsibility for Client Wrongs: Lehman Brothers and the Regulation of the Legal Profession' (2013) 76(1) *Modern Law Review* 26, 26.

public good. This gives them responsibility for important 'public values',[32] such as fairness and justice.

Lawyers are trained to study facts. Their knowledge of the law and legal duties informs their selection of relevant facts in clients' instructions. They also know how to find missing facts by using the legal processes of inter-rogatories and discovery. Lawyers learn to embrace, and the legal profession practises, 'hyper-rationality' in evaluating facts.[33] This strengthens the role of law in our conduct and supports the 'authority of legal reasoning'.[34] However, hyper-rationality may blunt moral sensitivity and discourage awareness of ethical issues.

Lawyers will use moral sensitivity to ascertain whether any of the moral virtues are being, or are likely to be, breached. Lawyers would then scrutinise clients' instructions to determine the ethicality of goals that lawyers' advice is meant to advance. Unethical client goals that drive clients' instructions could damage both lawyers and clients' reputations. Clients' goals are assessed by lawyers examining whether goals are just and fair, compassionate, and honest to the required standard.

Moral sensitivity helps lawyers better perform their professional obligations by revealing a need to closely scrutinise the potential impact of clients' goals. For example, as fiduciaries lawyers act in clients' best interests, but this ought not to include facilitating the clients' unethical goals or diminishing lawyers' professional integrity,

Step II: Moral Reasoning and Practical Wisdom

The aim of moral reasoning is for lawyers to think about and address the ethical issues identified in Step I. Moral reasoning includes the ethicality of clients' goals and their effect upon stakeholders of clients' decisions that are based upon lawyers' advice. Further, moral reasoning allows a moral judgement to be made, guided by Aristotelian and Kantian moral philosophies.

Practical wisdom evaluates how decisions may be implemented by deliberating upon 'both the ends and the means of practical conduct'.[35] Both moral reasoning and practical wisdom are relevant to lawyers when they give legal and ethical advice to clients. Both assist lawyers' duty to act in the best interests of their clients.

---

32 William Sullivan, *Work and Integrity: The Crisis and Promise of Professionalism in America* (Jossey-Bass, 2nd ed., 2005) 4.
33 Langevoort, above n 9, 118.
34 Ibid.
35 James Murphy, 'Practical Reason and Moral Psychology in Aristotle and Kant' (2001) 18(2) *Social Philosophy and Policy Foundation* 257, 259–60.

Enhancing Moral Reasoning and Practical Wisdom

Aristotle's intellectual virtues apply to moral reasoning. Aristotle uses them to determine the correct principle to regulate our conduct.[36] In addition, intellectual virtues contribute to character development that in turn relate to integrity, an important professional attribute. Intellectual virtues guide our choice of moral virtues.[37]

Kant has much to offer the process of moral reasoning as his philosophy exhibits similarities with lawyers' professional obligations. Duties arise from Kantian universal moral laws.[38] Kant says ethical conduct comes from our sense of obligation or duties to others[39] and that intelligence, reason, the will, and morality are linked.[40]

When the facts do not specifically relate to Kantian ethical duties, it is necessary to create a *maxim* to represent the proposed decision. The question now becomes: could we *will* (or wish) the decision to be a universal moral law? This is the process of universalisation. It examines the maxim and its likely outcomes in relation to achieving a goal. Another aspect of universalisation is that it relates to practical wisdom, that is, whether a decision could practically become a universal moral law.

Aristotle contributes to practical wisdom which he says refers to how a decision will be implemented, by establishing in a practical sense the achievement of the goals of moral virtues.[41] Aristotle argues that practical wisdom relates to justice and acts that benefit others. Further, these are indicators of a good person.[42] Practical wisdom has the flexibility to address both moral and intellectual virtues and arrive at a decision that is practical and possible to implement. This implementation is a test of character as we are morally accountable for our decisions. They must be implemented in a manner that is ethical, efficient, and timely.

Lawyers' Moral Reasoning and Practical Wisdom

Lawyers' moral reasoning should acknowledge our cognitive processes, such as reflective and reasoned thinking under system two thinking, that is

---

36 Aristotle, above n 22, 203.
37 Ibid.
38 Kant, above n 27, 21.
39 Ibid., 81.
40 Ibid.
41 Aristotle, above n 22, 222.
42 Ibid., 221.

more suitable for complex decisions.[43] Lawyers ought to consider factors that diminish our cognitive capacity, such as stress,[44] and its related issues of time deadlines and complexity of legal matters.

Moral reasoning includes drawing upon 'moral integrity to justify a particular line of action'.[45] For example, the issue could involve intended client conduct that is dishonest, such as misleading conduct, inadequate disclosure, or recklessness. These acts could relate to both law and ethics. They may not reach the threshold for illegality, but they are unethical.

Kantian duties and moral laws will inform lawyers' moral reasoning in the lawyer-to-client relationship. Kantian philosophy not only relates to lawyers' decisions concerning their clients, but it tells lawyers to ask the following duty-related questions in relation to the clients' stakeholders. First: are those affected by clients' decisions vulnerable persons? Second: are clients' decisions honest? Third: do these decisions respect persons?

The reasoning process for lawyers under the new model will include legal, professional, and moral reasoning as well as practical wisdom. In legal reasoning lawyers identify facts that relate to legal issues and then refer to sources of law (cases and statutes) to establish whether and how the law has been, or is likely to be, breached. Then, substantive legal reasoning is undertaken and used in lawyers' arguments supporting their interpretation of the law.

In professional reasoning, lawyers undertake a broader inquiry that evaluates the facts and the law and acknowledges lawyers' professional obligations: integrity, duties to the law and justice, and the fiduciary and confidentiality duties, as well as practical wisdom and judgement. Integrity is the personal filter through which professional obligations are interpreted and applied. Integrity is also supported by legal professional standards.[46]

Moral reasoning adds substance to professional obligations to give them a more explicitly ethical dimension. Lawyers' important duty to justice is at the heart of professional legal practice and moral judgement.[47] The ethical assessment involved in moral reasoning includes drawing upon 'role expectations'.[48] Every profession has an associated morality related to its

43 Bazerman and Tenbrunsel, above n 2, 153–4.
44 Langevoort, above n 9, 78.
45 Hutchinson, above n 21, 9.
46 *Legal Profession Uniform Law Act 2014* (NSW) s 126(a).
47 Lawrence Kohlberg and Richard Hersh, 'Moral Development: A Review of the Theory' (2001) Vol XVI (2) *Theory and Practice* 53, 56.
48 Hutchinson, above n 21, 9.

role. The new model of legal ethics expects lawyers as professionals to adopt a moral role in addition to their legal role. Indeed, statute adds a legal requirement to lawyers' role expectations as it says lawyers are 'to ensure appropriate safeguards are in place for maintaining the integrity of legal services'[49] and the integrity of the profession.[50] The meaning of integrity may be better appreciated by lawyers when Aristotelian and Kantian principles are applied under the new model.

Practical wisdom is acquired by lawyers' professional experience and judgement. It needs lawyers to assess whether their advice and the clients' implementation of it is practical in the context of the clients' business (or non-business). Lawyers must also appreciate important ideals in their clients' practice, whether (or not) it is a business, and consider these ideals when giving advice. For example, when legal advice was given to the Catholic Church regarding its response to sexual abuse, the impact of the lawyers' legal strategy was that it contributed to the Church's utter failure to exercise its duties of pastoral care toward the victims, opting instead for secrecy.[51]

One further matter lawyers must consider, before making the final decision upon which their advice is based, is moral imagination. This may be required to avoid unethical decisions being made by clients following legal advice.[52] This begins with an examination of an alternative course of action that clients may take that is ethical yet will still achieve clients' goals.

Before lawyers draft their advice, they must reflect on all parts of their decision-making process and make their final legal and ethical decisions the basis of their advice to clients. The following questions could assist lawyers' reflection: 'What does this decision say about the kind of person I am?'.[53] 'Would I be comfortable if my decision became public knowledge?'.[54] Reflection upon final decisions is a practical necessity. It involves whether all the relevant ethical and legal principles, and reasoning in Steps I and II that inform the lawyers' final advice, have been analysed in a manner that lawyers will be able to justify and explain in the dialogue with their clients.

---

49 *Legal Profession Uniform Law Act 2014* (NSW) s 126(a).
50 Ibid., s 423(2)(iv): authority for the *Legal Profession Uniform Law Australian Solicitors' Conduct Rules 2015* (NSW) see r 4, 5.
51 Robert Vischer, 'Legal Advice as Moral Perspective' (2006) 19 *Georgetown Journal of Legal Ethics* 225, 230.
52 Laura P Hartman, Joe Desjardins and Chris MacDonald, *Business Ethics: Decision-Making for Personal Integrity and Social Responsibility* (McGraw-Hill Irwin, 5th ed., 2021) 41.
53 Ibid., 89.
54 Richard de George, *Business Ethics* (Prentice Hall, 7th ed., 2010) 90.

Apply Steps I and II to James Hardie's Lawyers

Steps I and II of the new model are applied to key legal and ethical issues encountered by the law firm, Allens, in relation to its client James Hardie Industries Limited (JHIL). This practical example from corporate law practice gives us a better idea of the likely success of the new model. This was a tort case where former employees of James Hardie (JH) companies claimed compensation for the effects of work-related asbestos illness.

In February 2001, JHIL decided to restructure the group.[55] This included the issue of partly paid shares in JHIL[56] worth A$1.9 billion, that could be called upon to meet any future liability to tort claimants if funds for this purpose were depleted from the Medical Research and Compensation Fund (MRCF). This protection for tort victims was removed when those shares were cancelled, yet there was no guarantee of adequate funding for MRCF. This presented significant legal and ethical issues

A Supreme Court hearing was held in August 2001 to approve the restructure. The client, JHIL, and its lawyers, Allens, both had legal duties to disclose to the Court.[57] The client did not disclose its intention to cancel the partly paid shares, although it was formulated in early 2001 and effected in March 2003.[58] This lack of disclosure was found by Commissioner Jackson to be a breach by both JHIL and Allens of their legal duty to disclose to the Court, although in the case of Allens, this was not intentional.[59]

Core Principles of the New Model

Allens did not disclose to the Supreme Court as it 'had no reason to believe JHIL intended to cancel the shares'.[60] Allens said it relied upon written advice from JHIL directors, emails, JHIL board meetings, and its own notes.[61] The Commissioner disagreed with Allens's analysis.[62]

---

55 *Corporations Act 2001* (Cth) see Part 5.1 Arrangements and Reconstructions.
56 New South Wales, 'Special Commission of Inquiry into the Medical Research and Compensation Foundation' (Report, September 2004) David Jackson, QC, Commissioner ('*Jackson Report*') [25.5] 423. https://www.dpc.nsw.gov.au/publications/categories
57 Ibid., [25.35] 436.
58 *Australian Securities and Investments Commission v Macdonald (No 11)* [2009] NSWSC 287, alleged by ASIC, but unproven [1302] 341; *Jackson Report:* cancellation of the partly paid shares was an objective of the JH group, above n 56, [25.71] 451.
59 *Jackson Report,* above n 56, [25.91] 456.
60 Ibid., [25.59] 444.
61 Ibid., [25.81] 453.
62 Ibid., [25.87] 456.

If we take the Commissioner's view, then Allens's decision offends guiding *principle one* of the new model: the obligation of professional integrity where lawyers advance clients' interests within the bounds of law and morality. The interpretation by JHIL of its interests was not to disclose its intended share cancellation. This was both a legal and moral issue as tort claimants relied upon assurances given in Court, that these shares would offer them financial protection, if needed.

The client's cause to later deny this financial resource to claimants by cancelling these shares was unethical, and the lawyers' advancement of it was a breach of the model's guiding *principle two* of morality. Having applied the facts to the new model's guiding principles, lawyers then proceed to Steps I and II.

Step I: Moral Sensitivity

Moral sensitivity enables the identification of potential ethical issues. The significance of this is that some of these issues will also have legal consequences, while others will affect the reputation of lawyers or clients. In the JH case, the lawyers were blind to the full ethical implications of what the client was intending and they, as lawyers, were facilitating. Moral sensitivity is not part of positivist TLE and, therefore, it is reasonable to conclude it was not part of the lawyers' case preparation. With little moral sensitivity, there was less awareness on the part of the lawyers or identification of significant ethical issues that were a major part of this case. A morals-infused TLE would have produced a different outcome.

The consequence of a positivist TLE was that there was no foundation in the lawyer-to-client relationship, nor a requirement for lawyers to engage in moral reasoning. The lawyers continued to prepare their case for the restructure of the JH group, informed only by the law, without appreciating ethical concerns. This meant that the lawyers could not anticipate the outcomes for the client or themselves professionally. The effects of JHIL's unethical decisions were later revealed: denial of compensation for many former employees and future claimants suffering asbestos exposure-related illness.

Lawyers' Moral Sensitivity: Aristotelian Virtues and Kantian Duties

Aristotle's moral virtues of compassion, fairness, honesty, and the intellectual virtue of competence, tell us that, for ethical reasons, all tort victims with proven claims ought to receive compensation. Further, tort victims had trusted assurances from JHIL in Court that it would fulfil promises to compensate. Aristotle's moral virtue of fairness and Kant's duty of respect would both have given Allens a wider ethical context. The new model with its emphasis upon ethics, would have better informed these lawyers. They could have given ethical and legal advice, and in so doing reduced reputational damage to both themselves, and JHIL. The tort victims would have received the protection previously offered by the partly paid shares.

Kantian duties: to the vulnerable, honesty, and respect of persons, are also applicable. Asbestos claimants were vulnerable people as they depended upon JHIL's commitment to retain the partly paid shares. Failure to honour this commitment was dishonest and exploitative.

Strengthening Lawyers' Professional Obligations

Moral sensitivity would have alerted Allens that JHIL's strategy regarding the partly paid shares and lack of disclosure to the Court could be unethical and illegal for both JHIL and Allens. This required a close examination by Allens of its client's actions to be able to advise them.

Moral sensitivity would have contributed to Allens's awareness that if the ethical concerns became a reality, as ethical breaches, this would impact upon Allens's professional integrity and have legal significance. Ethical breaches could also be breaches of lawyers' primary professional duties to the law and justice, and the duty of disclosure. However, without moral principles in positivist TLE, lawyers tend to direct their attention only to the law and the client's narrative of the facts. A new legal ethics with moral sensitivity, would give lawyers a broader understanding and bolster professional commitments.

Step II: Moral Reasoning and Practical Wisdom

Moral reasoning is important as it leads to lawyers' final decision that informs their advice to clients. Aristotle argues that what we choose to do is significant as it relates to good character and integrity,[63] the foundation of Aristotelian philosophy.[64] Moral reasoning reflects choices we have made to arrive at a judgement.

Lawyers' Moral Reasoning: Aristotelian Virtues and Kantian Duties

Allens informed the Supreme Court it 'had no reason to believe JHIL intended to cancel the shares'.[65] Commissioner Jackson found that Allens

---

63 Aristotle, above n 22, 115.
64 Ibid., 90.
65 *Jackson Report,* above n 56, [25.59] 444.

did have prior knowledge of the share cancellation as it was 'familiar with JHIL's internal strategic planning' and knew 'the true purpose of the partly paid shares – stakeholder management – [and] would have formed the view that their cancellation was almost inevitable'.[66] The Commissioner found that Allens chose to confine its 'area of inquiry [in relation to what had to be disclosed] to the period from March 2001', a period that JHIL's board had decided 'did not need to be disclosed'.[67] Commissioner Jackson said it had been inappropriate for Allens to confine its inquiry in this way.[68] (The illegality studied here, is the failure by Allens to disclose to the Court the likelihood of cancellation, not the eventual cancellation of the partly paid shares, as this was legal.)

Under Kantian duties, a lack of disclosure by Allens was unethical showing a lack of respect for Santow J of the Supreme Court, JHIL members, and the tort victims. The failure to disclose resulted in the restructure's approval of an illusory protection for shareholders and tort claimants. If Allens had known of the possibility of the share cancellation, which it claimed it did not, its decision not to disclose would have been unethical. This would have constituted a breach of both the ethical duties of honesty and respect regarding the group's vulnerable former employees (and later, those outsiders such as tradespeople, who were the consumers of JH's products).

Kant also determines ethicality by an appeal to universal moral laws. Analysing decisions in this manner clarifies their ethicality. The maxim in relation to Allens's decision not to disclose what Commissioner Jackson said were relevant matters to the Court, could be this: 'In order to achieve a client's goal, a lawyer may make a representation to court on the client's behalf without investigating its veracity'. Kant would then examine the effect of this maxim and determine whether it could apply as a moral law universally to every lawyer. This maxim would mean that lawyers would lose their integrity, a vital part of lawyers' professionalism. This loss of integrity and professionalism would seriously erode client and community trust in the truth of lawyers' representations. While the benefit of supporting this maxim would be to satisfy certain clients' wishes, the detriment to lawyers personally and professionally, would be too great. Therefore, this maxim would offend Kant's Categorical Imperative and could not be a universal moral law.

66 Ibid., [25.87] 456.
67 Ibid., [25.82] 455.
68 Ibid.

Lawyers' Practical Wisdom

Allens's reflection upon practical matters would have primarily concerned its decision to accept JHIL's position that no disclosure to the Court was required. Here, the interaction of the law and ethics was important for Allens. The restructure was approved by the Supreme Court in 2001.[69] The partly paid shares were cancelled 18 months later, in 2003.[70] The Court had been given an assurance that tort claimants were financially protected by the shares, therefore, once this protection was removed, some other suitable arrangement had to replace it.[71] It was not until 2006 that this was achieved in a settlement involving the NSW State Government.[72]

It appears that Allens followed JHIL's advice that there was nothing to disclose to the Court. However, perhaps Allens could have looked more closely at JHIL's internal strategic planning to find the motivation driving its plan to cancel the partly paid share issue. This appears to be what Commissioner Jackson expected and why he did not agree with Allens's reasons for the lack of disclosure. When Allens accepted JHIL's advice that disclosure to the Court of the cancellation plans was not necessary, this decision was not practical as it had legal consequences for JHIL and for Allens, as well as professional consequences.

Strengthening Lawyers' Professional Obligations

Positivist TLE's absence of moral sensitivity and moral reasoning resulted in Allens having no reason to evaluate the facts from an ethical perspective of virtues and duties. Allens was, therefore, disadvantaged by the current client-centred positivist TLE where lawyers' professional independence from clients is diminished. This can lead to lawyers being 'captured' by clients' imperatives, commercial and otherwise, as well as clients' lack of ethical engagement. Allens would have been under pressure to meet deadlines and the demands of JHIL as a client. These factors reduce our cognitive capacity and increase the likelihood of less reflective (system one) thinking. Allens may not have given enough thought to its own legal position

---

69 *Jackson Report,* above n 56, [25.26] 433.

70 Ibid., [26.67] 512.

71 *Corporations Act 2001* (Cth) s 256B.

72 James Hardie Industries NV, *Explanatory Memorandum: Proposal to Provide Long-Term Funding for Compensating Australian Asbestos-Related Personal Injury Claims against Former James Hardie Companies,* 12 December 2006, Part B, [1.2] 2. https://ir.jameshardie.com.au/public/download.jsp?id=2054

before it breached its duty of disclosure to the Supreme Court. Significantly, Commissioner Jackson found Allens's actions were not deliberate.[73]

The new model of TLE envisages an independent, moral, and legal role for lawyers. It provides the means to bring ethics into the decision-making process. In the JH case, lawyers' use of moral sensitivity would have identified the ethical issues in relation to the client's conduct and their own. This ethical awareness would have revealed to Allens that they were unintentionally facilitating the client's unethical decisions to their own (and the client's) legal detriment.

Step III: Dialogue with Clients

Here, lawyers explain and endeavour to persuade clients regarding the ethical and legal issues in their advice. The dialogue will assist clients to make the ethical and legal decisions recommended by their lawyers. The dialogue is informed by Steps I and II including the legal practice issues where Aristotelian and Kantian principles are applied. Lawyers need to be motivated to take the action their decisions require, as they are accountable both legally and morally under the core principles of the new model of legal ethics. Moral conviction is important as it gives 'priority to the decided-on moral course of action over other values or goals' such as either clients or lawyers' self-interest.[74]

The ethical position is that lawyers' advice must take heed of the impact of clients' decisions on stakeholders when clients act upon lawyers' advice. Lawyers are ethically accountable for two categories of decisions. The first is their own decisions and how these affect their clients as clients are the lawyers' stakeholders. The second is their clients' decisions and how they affect creditors, employees, shareholders, and consumers, all of whom are the clients' stakeholders. If the clients' decisions can be linked to their lawyers' advice, then lawyers are indirect stakeholders of their clients.

The legal position for lawyers is they could be breaching their duty to clients. In addition, they could be joined with clients as parties involved in their clients' contravention of the law. The JH case shows how corporate lawyers could be implicated. Allens was instructed by JHIL's directors who, it appears, permitted JHIL to breach its duty to disclose to the Court. This was a breach of directors' fiduciary duty to JHIL.[75] In addition, Allens also owed a fiduciary duty to JHIL, its client, and in this capacity, Allens needed

---

73 *Jackson Report,* above n 56, [25.91] 456.

74 Hutchinson, above n 21, 9.

75 *Corporations Act 2001* (Cth) s 181(1)(a).

to advise JHIL that it had a disclosure duty. Allens also could have breached the law as persons involved in the directors' contravention.[76]Further, shareholders may bring proceedings on behalf of a company in relation to the conduct of the affairs of the company, if the company fails to initiate proceedings against its directors.[77]

Explanation to and Persuasion of Clients

It is an important service to clients for lawyers to explain their written advice before it is formalised in a final advice document. Lawyers do this by revealing the legal principles that support the advice and its implementation. This is the usual dialogue lawyers already have with their clients. Under the new model, lawyers will also explain relevant ethical principles.

'Persuasion' refers to *how* lawyers explain their advice to clients. Lawyers' knowledge of our cognitive processes and biases will influence the dialogue as these exist in all of us, lawyers and clients alike. This understanding will highlight the type of explanation lawyers need to give clients to encourage them to accept their advice. This will make lawyers' dialogue more meaningful. This dialogue is significant for lawyers' own decisions and those of their clients.

Lawyers' advice ought to include matters of moral responsibility that require them to adopt two new responsibilities.[78] The first is to explicitly state the 'moral dimensions' of the legal conduct they are advising clients to undertake.[79] The second is to advise clients that they, the clients, need to evaluate these moral dimensions to see how they align with their own 'institutional values' (or personal values).[80] It is useful, if clients are not readily persuaded by lawyers' advice, for clients to be reminded that their lawyers' advice if viewed objectively, comes within the values of the clients' business or institution. This is also the context of client instructions.

Usually, clients engage lawyers to give legal advice that has the purpose of reassuring clients that their goals and strategies, to realise them, are legal. However, if client goals and/or strategies are legal but unethical, and lawyers' formal advice is used to facilitate these strategies by legal means, it may raise professional issues. This situation is one of the dilemmas that

76 Ibid., s 181(2); s 79.
77 Ibid., ss 236(1), 237(2).
78 Tony Foley, 'Institutional Responses to Child Sexual Abuse: How a Moral Conversation with its Lawyers might Contribute to Cultural Change in a Faith-Based Institution' (2015) 18(2) *Legal Ethics* 164, 180.
79 Ibid.
80 Ibid., 180.

the new model of legal ethics seeks to resolve by bringing ethics into legal ethics so that lawyers give both ethical and legal advice to clients.

If lawyers believe clients may use their advice to further their goals at the risk of illegal or unethical conduct, lawyers must suggest alternative courses of action to the advice to remove these risks. In ethics, this is called using 'moral imagination'.[81] Lawyers can assist clients by using moral imagination and persuading them to accept amendments to the advice that will still satisfy their objectives but will also meet the community's ethical expectations. Legal imagination is possible, too, if there are other parts of the law that better achieve clients' goals.

Asserting Lawyers' Professional Independence

Lawyers now move from persuasion to impartial professionalism with the moral courage required of professionals. This change of attitude could be expressed to the client as a type of gatekeeper role, one that is particularly relevant for corporate lawyers.[82] Here, lawyers advise clients that this role is activated if they intend to use lawyers' advice to make decisions that either impact lawyers' professional integrity, or lawyers' legal duties to the law and justice. Lawyers, as professionals and with a moral role under the new model, cannot afford to be implicated in or contribute to, illegal or unethical decisions of clients that challenge their lawyers' professional obligations.

The JH case is a good example of the issues faced by corporate lawyers. Here, JHIL was a powerful client that would probably *not* have been persuaded by their lawyers even if moral imagination was offered. The parent company wanted to restructure the group and it could legally do so. However, the major issue in this case was the impact of this legal decision. It led to unethical consequences that created a funding shortfall for injured workers. Under the new model Allens could have asserted their professional independence. This would have been a very difficult conversation for them with JHIL, their long-standing client. However, in a lawyer-to-client relationship, JHIL could not have expected an unbroken record of acquiescence by its lawyers to their demands.

Lawyers' professional and legal duties require lawyers to avoid involvement in their clients' illegal acts.[83] Further, lawyers cannot advise clients

---

81 de George, above n 54, 90.
82 John C Coffee Jr, *Gatekeepers: The Professions and Corporate Governance* (Oxford University Press, 2006).
83 G E Dal Pont, *Lawyers' Professional Responsibility* (Thomson Reuters, 7th ed., 2021) [19.10] 654.

if lawyers reasonably believe the advice could contribute to an illegal purpose.[84] These matters also breach *principle one* of the new model regarding professional integrity. Therefore, lawyers can refuse to act for their clients[85] where clients ask lawyers to act unethically, or client conduct using lawyers' advice is likely to implicate lawyers, then lawyers must evaluate the personal and professional ethical risks to their integrity.

Professional independence involves defending one's integrity and professionalism. This comes at a price but there are also rewards, the most important of which are lawyers' self-respect and their clients' respect. This is valuable because lawyers are then regarded by clients as true professionals, not mere mouthpieces or service providers.

The new moral model of legal ethics restores lawyers' independence. Although the client is the contractual party and the principal to whom the fiduciary duty is owed, this is balanced with the independence that lawyers require to uphold their other professional obligations: duties to the law and justice, and the public good. The new model will give lawyers the additional guidance and support they require to stand up to clients and protect their own professionalism.

Conclusion

The new moral model of legal ethics places ethics at the forefront by applying the philosophies of Aristotle and Kant. The model supports an increased emphasis upon the importance of ethics and a moral role for all lawyers. Lawyers 'must describe the ethical choices robustly' and 'can no longer cast themselves just as the ministrants of law' as *lawyers must be moral leaders.*[86] It is a reasonable expectation for lawyers to have a moral role as clients' decisions often adversely affect many stakeholders. Lawyers' public duties to the law and to justice as well as the integrity of the profession, justify this expectation.

Lawyers also should be aware of our cognitive processes and which parts of legal practice typically trigger them. Lawyers must be proactive, as indicated in Steps I and II, and in their dialogue with clients. Under the new model, lawyers could become more ethically sensitive and undertake moral reasoning, thus enhancing their ability to participate in the more reflective system two thinking.

---

84 Ibid., [19.50] 659.
85 Ibid., [19.10] 654.
86 Philip R. Wood, *The Fall of the Priests and the Rise of the Lawyers* (Hart Publishing Ltd, 2016) 253, emphasis added.

The new model gives lawyers much needed independence from their clients to objectively address both legal and ethical issues in their advice and subsequent dialogue with clients. This is more likely to benefit clients. If lawyers do this then, they would have done all that one could expect of them. They have analysed the ethical and legal issues and presented these to the clients. It is then the clients' responsibility whether they choose to follow either part of their lawyers' advice.

8 Conclusion

Legal ethics has two limbs, theoretical legal ethics (TLE), and lawyers' professional obligations. Their significance is that both limbs impact legal practice. The new moral model of TLE is a necessary reform for the legal profession. This enables lawyers to consider ethical issues in clients' instructions and give ethical as well as legal advice. Lawyers' moral TLE is important as its principles extend lawyers' role to one that concerns the law *and* ethics. Further, these principles influence lawyers' performance of their professional obligations.

In many ways, the law is what lawyers want to make it when they interpret and apply it. Ethical ideals of fairness and honesty are embedded in law. However, this is not enough to balance ethical deficiencies in positivist TLE. Lawyers are more than mere interpreters of the law as designated by a positivist TLE. Lawyers are professionals in whom the public place their trust. This bestows upon them an ethical role that the moral TLE will assist lawyers to achieve. Lawyers will more successfully meet their own and the public's perception of what the legal profession stands for: their clients, professional values, and the public interest as filtered by the concerns of justice. The logic of the arguments in this book is summarised here.

- Lawyers' current TLE, the first limb of legal ethics, was developed in the 19th century, and suited legal practice in this period. This is far too narrow for modern legal practice in the 21st century. This model tells lawyers they are more like 'political officials than … ordinary moral agents'[1] as reflected in positivist TLE's principles of partisanship and moral neutrality.[2] This limb of legal ethics directly influences the second limb.

---

1 W Bradley Wendel, *Lawyers and Fidelity to Law* (Princeton University Press, 2010) 7–8.
2 Ibid., 6.

DOI: 10.4324/9781003264286-8

- Lawyers' performance of their professional obligations is the second limb of legal ethics. Here, lawyers are to concern themselves with the law and 'not aim directly at justice' nor 'make [ethical] decisions in the same way morally reflective people' do.[3] If justice is not well served, this undercuts the raison d'être of the legal profession. Ignoring ethical issues sometimes has ethical as well as legal consequences for both lawyers and clients as we saw in the James Hardie (JH) case study. The ethical content within lawyers' duties to the law and to justice is a context for lawyers acting in the public good.[4] This professional issue provides the continuing justification of all professions.[5]

- Another consequence of the current TLE is that lawyers cannot give clients ethical advice, even if it is in the clients' best interests to do so. This may have a negative influence upon lawyers' fiduciary duty. It is argued in this book that positivist TLE may cause lawyers to breach this duty when ethical advice *is* in the best interests of clients.

- There is a personal effect upon lawyers as a consequence of the role prescribed for them under positivist TLE. Lawyers are aware that the diminution of ethics in their role may raise questions of their professional integrity, thus distinguishing 'lawyers from other professionals'.[6] This is unfair and a disservice to lawyers.

Legal Ethics and Legal Practice

The above arguments point to practical problems for lawyers with a positivist TLE. It guides lawyers in their interpretation of the nature, scope, and effect of their professional obligations, whether these are legal or ethical. This in turn informs lawyers when they advise clients.

Over the last 50 years, legal practice has become much more sophisticated. Accordingly, the law has increased in complexity to address these developments. However, there remain ethical gaps in the way client strategies are employed and what the law will permit. The JH case is an example of this. The client was able to bring its strategies within the law while making decisions that were unethical and unfair for stakeholders. Positivist TLE had no answer for this injustice and, consequently, neither did the client,

---

3   Ibid., 208.
4   James Allsop, 'Professionalism and Commercialism: Conflict or Harmony in Modern Legal Practice?' (2010) 84 *Australian Law Journal* 765, 765–6.
5   Richard Moorhead, 'Precarious Professionalism: Some Empirical and Behavioural Perspectives on Lawyers' (2014) 67 *Current Legal Problems* 447, 450–1.
6   Richard Wasserstrom, 'Lawyers as Professionals: Some Moral Issues' (1975) 5(1) *Human Rights* 1, 14.

James Hardie Industries Limited (JHIL), nor its external lawyers, Allens who had to fulfil the role specified by positivist TLE: to advise clients only upon the law.

In the JH case, JHIL's lawyers, Allens, unintentionally breached its legal duty of disclosure to the court[7] when it relied upon assurances from JHIL. Positivist TLE encourages such reliance while it contemporaneously limits lawyers' professional independence from clients. Overreliance by lawyers upon clients neither assists them nor their clients. Paradoxically it is not helping lawyers or clients to uphold the law: the core principle of positivist TLE. The public was outraged at JHIL's decisions concerning tort claimants. Some of this public anger was directed at JHIL's lawyers as it appeared that legal advice had sanctioned JHIL's conduct. This places lawyers under personal and professional stress.

Some supporters of positivist TLE admit that at least a few lawyers have reacted to positivist TLE by stretching and manipulating the law and that this is currently acceptable legal practice by some lawyers.[8] This stretches the meaning of 'professional' obligations to breaking point. There is a personal toll upon lawyers in this situation, whether lawyers engage in this conduct, merely contemplate it, or observe it in other lawyers. Where does this leave lawyers professionally in view of their professional obligations to the law? In the absence of morality in positivist TLE, lawyers may perceive their role as that of 'amoral technicians',[9] a role that no lawyer would want professionally or personally.

The close connection between lawyers' TLE and lawyers' professional obligations is that both are integral to legal practice, yet there is a tension between positivist TLE and professional obligations. The latter has both a legal and ethical orientation: professional integrity, law and justice, fiduciary and confidentiality duties, and acting in the public good. Whereas positivist TLE appears to contradict this by telling lawyers they must advise upon and uphold the law (including their own legal duties), while at the same time separating ethics from the law. This separation removes serious ethical reflection and the important role it could have in giving ethical support to clarify and enhance lawyers' professional obligations.

---

7 New South Wales, Special Commission of Inquiry into the Medical Research and Compensation Foundation, *Report by Commissioner David Jackson QC* (September 2004) ('Jackson Report') [25.91] 456. https://www.dpc.nsw.gov.au/publications/categories

8 Stephen L Pepper, 'The Lawyer Knows More than the Law' (2012) 90(3) *Texas Law Review* 691, 692.

9 Robert Vischer, 'Legal Advice as Moral Perspective' (2006) 19 *Georgetown Journal of Legal Ethics* 225, 228.

The Role of Moral Philosophy

A consideration of the most relevant moral principles to be brought into legal ethics concluded that the moral philosophies of Aristotle and Kant were the most appropriate for the legal profession. When they were studied individually and together, it was found there was symmetry between them. Further, their principles could be applied to bring morals into lawyers' TLE, as well as addressing the moral underpinnings of lawyers' professional duties. It was concluded these philosophies would more clearly promote the high moral standard that society expects of lawyers, where morals are essential in the professional endeavour.[10]

Professional integrity, an overarching requirement for lawyers, and their most important professional obligation, is about honesty and consistency in both deeds and principles.[11] Acts of integrity are the heart of professional ethics because integrity is what professionals believe in, practice, and profess to live by.[12] Aristotle's moral virtue of honesty and Kant's duty of honesty both support professional integrity. The driving force of Aristotelian philosophy is character development,[13] and this too is a basis of integrity.[14] Kantian philosophy also examines character as it relates to our will, this being a major principle in his philosophy.[15]

Lawyers' professional duties acknowledge that everything in legal practice is shaped by lawyers' duties to the law and justice. Aristotle relates justice to character and implies that persons of good character value justice and uphold the moral virtues of honesty, courage, and compassion to satisfy the principles of justice: moral rightness and fairness.[16] Lawyers' fiduciary duty to act in the best interests of their clients is supported by the Kantian duties to assist vulnerable people and to uphold the dignity of man.[17] Together these duties support the vulnerability principle within the fiduciary duty.

10 Max Weber, *The Protestant Ethic and the Spirit of Capitalism* (Talcott Parsons trans., Unwin University Books, 1930) 79–80.

11 David Luban, 'Integrity: Its Causes and Cures' (2003) 72(2/4) *Fordham Law Review* 279, 279.

12 Hugh Breakey, 'Compromise Despite Conviction: Curbing Integrity's Moral Dangers' (2016) 50(3) *Journal of Value Inquiry* 613, 621.

13 Aristotle, *The Ethics of Aristotle: The Nicomachean Ethics* (J A K Thomson trans., Penguin Books, 1976) 90.

14 Sharon Dolovich, 'Ethical Lawyering and the Possibility of Integrity' (2002) 70 *Fordham Law Review* 1629, 1631.

15 Immanuel Kant, *Foundations of the Metaphysics of Morals* (Lewis White Beck trans., Bobbs-Merrill, 1978) 11

16 Aristotle, above n 13, 171.

17 Kant, above n 15, 54.

The clarification and enrichment given by Aristotelian and Kantian principles to the professional obligations of integrity and duties to the law and justice support the use of these principles in lawyers' professional obligations. The interpretative function of these philosophies enables lawyers to better appreciate the existing ethical content within their professional obligations. This will benefit both lawyers and clients.

The Originality of the New Legal Ethics Model

Legal ethics under the new model now tells lawyers that they have a moral role in addition to interpreting the law. It provides that lawyers have independence from clients, and that lawyers objectively uphold their professional obligations giving clients both legal and ethical advice.

The foundation principles of the new moral model of TLE are the primary obligation of professional integrity, the principle of morality, and the principle of accountability. These principles constitute an infusion of ethics into TLE and lawyers' professional obligations.

Step I: Moral Sensitivity, is about giving lawyers moral awareness as professionals. This is the ability to recognise and identify ethical issues in client instructions. While their personal ethics may alert lawyers to an ethical issue, their legal ethics does not address this. Lawyers are trained to study the law, as well as legally relevant facts. However, part of the factual matrix often includes ethical issues. A knowledge of the basic concepts in applied Aristotelian and Kantian philosophies will assist lawyers to develop moral awareness.

Step II: Moral Reasoning and Practical Wisdom, requires lawyers to act upon ethical issues identified in Step I, by analysing them with close attention to Aristotelian and Kantian reasoning. These philosophies consider practical wisdom too, that is, how a decision will be implemented. Moral reasoning adds substance to professional obligations to give them a more explicitly ethical dimension.

The new model provides lawyers with the best opportunity when they prepare their formal advice, to assist clients to reach their goals in an ethical and a legal manner. This advice later becomes the subject of lawyers' dialogue with clients. Lawyers' advice may suggest to clients that they use moral imagination as this examines alternative courses of action to achieve the same client objectives whilst also considering the ethical aspects of their strategies.

Step III: Dialogue with Clients, requires lawyers to work to persuade clients to consider accepting more broadly based advice that addresses both legal and ethical matters. Lawyers are in a unique position to counsel clients on underlying ethical problems that may arise from clients' proposed decisions. Lawyers could point out to clients that ethical advice is often in their best interests. The JH case study showed this. Lawyers could persuade clients by pointing to the consequences for clients of ignoring ethical advice.

Clients need to appreciate the social, reputational, and financial advantages to them of being ethical and being seen to be ethical. Stakeholder loyalty is something clients cannot afford to put at risk. After all, clients' stakeholders may be their employees (as in the JH case), creditors, or customers, all of whom have potential and actual relationships with these clients.

Some clients may choose not to follow their lawyers' ethical advice even if this results in exposing themselves to reputational and financial risks. Similarly, some clients may not follow their lawyers' legal advice although this is less likely as here clients will incur more immediate sanctions for legal breaches. In both situations, once lawyers have given clients their formal advice, they will have fulfilled their responsibilities under legal ethics and professionally because they will have complied with the new model of TLE and their professional obligations.

The new model of legal ethics gives lawyers greater independence from clients by becoming the independent professionals they are meant to be. This makes it easier for lawyers to provide objective expert advice on the law and ethics. This greater independence made possible by the model also gives lawyers a unique opportunity to assist clients and support the public good by undertaking an ethical gatekeeper role. Clients' consideration of stakeholders affected by their decisions following lawyers' advice, is one of the purposes of the dialogue with clients. Unethical decisions of clients are usually not discovered by stakeholders until it is too late both for them and the clients whose reputations are now tarnished.

In the JH case, it was possible to predict (what, indeed turned out to be) the outcome of a funding shortfall for asbestos claimants. This included dissatisfied workers, community outrage, and a state government prepared to initiate an inquiry into this funding.[18] This inquiry cost JH in reputation and time spent over months by its lawyers and executives in preparing for and giving testimony before the Commission.

Significance of the New Legal Ethics Model

One consequence of clients using lawyers' advice to make unethical decisions is that it may generate a perception that lawyers 'participate in

---

18 *Jackson Report,* above n 7.

injustice'.[19] This gives the impression that lawyers lack professionalism, which is untrue and unfair. However, a distinguished legal theorist noted 'a prevailing climate of ethical ambivalence and professional indifference' amongst lawyers.[20] This statement was made in relation to litigation lawyers but may also apply to transactional lawyers:

> Lawyers are not only portrayed as skilled at the dubious arts of manipulation and double dealing, but also castigated as *moral hypocrites* because they defend these practices in the brazen name *of 'professional ethics'*.[21]

This is not an isolated criticism but part of a long history of similar statements by others. Some of the lay public have unfortunate perceptions of the legal profession where members' own misdeeds or involvement in poor decision-making by clients have been sensationalised by the media. This reinforces these negative opinions. These are public perceptions, not reality. Nevertheless, they are important as they are relevant to lawyers' integrity, sense of self (self-identity), and reputation.

One of the main elements of reputation is perceived personal and professional integrity, yet less than 20 per cent of the public in a similar jurisdiction to Australia are confident that lawyers have professional integrity.[22] There is a way to improve this perception, and this is to encourage lawyers' moral independence from clients, and to recognise the role of ethical principles as also being in the public interest. In many ways, the law is what lawyers want to make it when they interpret and apply the law. Ethics within the law is not enough to balance ethical deficiencies in positivist TLE. This is the significance of the new model of legal ethics.

The adoption of the new model will succeed if it receives recognition by professional bodies and tertiary institutions. This will only occur after these organisations accept that positivist TLE is inadequate and could be enriched by the new ethical model; and further, that this model would advance the standing of the profession in the community.

19 William Simon, *The Practice of Justice: A Theory of Lawyers' Ethics* (Harvard University Press, 1998) 109.
20 Allan Hutchinson, *Fighting Fair: Legal Ethics for an Adversarial Age* (Cambridge University Press, 2015) 21.
21 Ibid., 1–2 (emphasis added).
22 Deborah Rhode, *In the Interests of Justice: Reforming the Legal Profession* (Oxford University Press, 2000) 208. Rhode refers to American lawyers, but it could be assumed that there would be a similar result in Australia.

In terms of practical steps forward, lawyers' professional bodies could include annual ethics seminars on the application of this model. The seminars designed for in-house and law firm lawyers could award them mandatory continuing legal education credits. Law societies already have ethics seminars and major law firms have in-house ethics seminars, but these are not based upon a model of legal ethics that overtly supports ethics and provides ethical reasoning informed by moral philosophies. Rather, they are founded upon hypothetical scenarios without a model of legal ethics that provides the ethical analyses and processes found in Steps I and II of the new model. The benefit of knowing how to resolve a described ethical situation in a hypothetical one does not translate to the unique factual scenarios faced by lawyers in clients' instructions. Lawyers should have a structured guide to assist them in advising clients, whatever the factual scenario.

The essence of the above arguments is that lawyers' professionalism may be at risk. The elements of true professionalism include excellence in knowledge and high standards in its application. Equally important is a passionate belief in legal practice and the values represented by it.[23] The moral philosophies of Aristotle and Kant as part of both limbs of legal ethics, will take lawyers closer to realising the ideal of the true professional: a competent expert whose values and performance are honourable. Our clients expect nothing less from us.

---

23 David Maister, *True Professionalism: The Courage to Care About Your People, Your Clients, and Your Career* (The Free Press, 1997) 11.

Index

Note: Page numbers followed by "n" indicate endnotes.

Abel, R. 60
ABN 60 Pty Ltd ('ABN 60') 26
Allens (Arthur Robinson, Solicitors)
  20; breaching legal duty of
  disclosure in JH case 111–13, 119;
  and Kantian philosophy 91; lack of
  disclosure by 110; moral reasoning
  109–10; principles of positivist
  TLE 63; professional independence
  under new model of legal ethics 114;
  professional obligation to justice
  88; response to ASX announcement
  83–4; restructure of JH group 94;
  see also lawyer-to-client relationship
  between Allens and JHIL
Allsop, J. 9–11, 118
Amaba Pty Ltd (Amaba) 20, 38, 64;
  JHIL's decision to separate from
  26, 29, 30; and JHI NV 43; legal
  avenues for former employees of 45;
  tort liabilities for 21, 23–5
Amaca Pty Ltd (Amaca) 38, 64; JHIL's
  decision to separate from 26, 29,
  30; and JHI NV 43; legal avenues
  for former employees of 45; tort
  liabilities for 21, 23–5
amoral technicians 59, 61, 119
Aristotelian philosophy 68–9, 109;
  Aristotelian ethics 84; character
  development 70–1, 86, 120; fiduciary
  and confidentiality duties 90–1; and
  integrity 81–2; intellectual virtues
  71–2, 104; lawyers' duties to law and
justice 86–7; lawyers' knowledge
  in 121; moral sensitivity 102; moral
  virtues 71–3, 82, 84, 88, 90, 93,
  94, 108–11; our choices 72, 102;
  practical wisdom 72–3, 92–3; virtues
  and excellence 71; *see also* Kantian
  philosophy
Arjoon, S. 79, 82
asbestos 20–2, 32; claimants 29, 109,
  122; claims 22, 31, 39–41; tort
  liability 20–6; tort victims 83
Asbestos Injuries Compensation Fund
  Ltd 45
Asbestos Mines Pty Ltd (Asbestos) 25
Austin, R. 29, 37
Australian Securities and Investments
  Commission v Hellicar 27, 33–4,
  36–7, 40, 64, 83, 107
Australian Securities and Investments
  Commission v Macdonald 33
Australian Securities Exchange (ASX)
  27, 83; announcement regarding
  MRCF's establishment 32–4, 83;
  disclosure obligation 32; JHIL's
  external lawyers and ASX disclosure
  35–6
automatic thinking 99

Bagust, J. 7, 16, 18
'Banking Royal Commission' *see*
  Commonwealth Royal Commission
  (Australia)
Bazerman, M. 98–100, 105

behavioural ethics 13, 98
Bell Group Ltd (in liq.) v Westpac
  Banking Corporation (No. 9) 30, 34
Breakey, H. 79–80, 120
Briggs v James Hardie & Co Pty Ltd 25
Brunninghausen v Glavonics 28

categorical imperative (Kant) 74,
  93, 110
Chan, J., 10character development 70,
  71, 81, 86, 104, 120
Chellew, J. 8–9, 16, 19
clients: dialogue with 98, 112–15,
  121–2; engaging in unethical
  conduct 101–3; lawyers and 14–19,
  88–91; lawyers' ethical advice
  to 57–70, 80, 82, 99; loyalty 86;
  persuasion of 113–14; principles of
  positivist TLE 53–4; protected by
  lawyers' fiduciary duty 76; reason for
  seeking legal opinion 2; rely upon
  ethical concepts 6; single-minded
  pursuit of different goals 5
clients' interests 54, 58, 60, 85, 89, 96,
  108; contradict community interest
  71; lawyers' obligation to regard 48;
  legal and commercial interests 58,
  60, 89; positivists' client-centred
  view with 47
client supremacy 1, 50, 51, 53, 60, 66;
  and lawyers' professional duties
  60–1; and legal practice 61–3;
  positivist TLE principles of 88
Coe, C. 14, 17, 19
Coffee, J. 90, 114
cognitive capacity: factors diminishing
  99–101; of lawyers 100
cognitive processes 98–101, 104,
  113, 115
Cohen, S. 79
Commonwealth Royal Commission
  (Australia) into 'Misconduct in
  the Banking, Superannuation
  and Financial Services Industry'
  (Final Report, 2019) Hayne, K.,
  Commissioner 14; *see also* 'Banking
  Royal Commission'
company law 14–15, 29, 43, 45
confidentiality duties 7, 10–11, 88, 105,
  119; Aristotelian philosophy 90–1;

Kantian philosophy 91; lawyers 89;
  positivist philosophy 89–90
corporate clients 14, 16, 18–19, 45–6
corporate lawyers 52; and clients
  14–15; external 16–19; in-house
  15–16; problem for 62, 90, 99
Corporations Act (C'th) Australia 15
courage 68, 71, 73, 81–2, 90, 102, 120
creditors 29, 82; future tort 30, 43, 44
CSR Ltd v Wren 25

Dal Pont, G. 8–9, 60, 63, 85, 90,
  114–15
Daniels v Anderson 23
Dare, T. 62, 80
Darvall v North Sydney Brick & Tile
  Co. Ltd 28–30
decision-making 76; ethical 13,
  50, 101; process of Kantian
  philosophy 36
De George, R. 67, 69, 76
dialogue with clients 112, 121–2;
  asserting lawyers' professional
  independence 114–15; explanation to
  and persuasion of 113–14
Dierksmeier, C. 73–4
dishonesty 75, 87
Dolovich, S. 85, 120
Donoghue v Stevenson 21
Duties: to help others 75; of honesty
  74–5, 82, 87, 97, 110, 120; Kant
  ethics 68–9; of respect 76, 84, 87,
  108–9

Edwards v Attorney General (NSW) 43
'equity acts on conscience' maxim 11
ethical/ethics 8, 11, 13, 53, 90; blind
  spots 13, 98; decision-making 13,
  50, 101; in lawyers' advice 57–60; in
  legal practice 56–7; separation 53–5;
  see also legal ethics
ethicality delusion 98–9
Ethics of Aristotle: the Nicomachean
  Ethics 69
Evans, A. 16, 18, 30, 52, 84–5
excellence of action 71, 102, 124
Ex Parte Lenehan 79
expertise of lawyers in law 8, 10, 15,
  57, 68, 93, 97
explanatory memorandum 38, 45

external corporate law firm 20
external corporate lawyers 16–19
external lawyers 15–16; conflicts of
    interest 18–19; of JHIL and ASX
    disclosure 35–6; of JHIL and MRCF
    42–3; and restructure 27; tort
    liabilities and restructure 27–8
extra-legal conceptions of morality
    59–60

fairness 9, 81, 86, 88, 102–3, 108,
    117, 120
fidelity to law 55–6, 58, 61
fiduciaries lawyers 103
fiduciary duties 1, 2, 7, 10–11, 61, 77,
    88, 105, 119; Aristotelian philosophy
    90–1; Kantian philosophy 91;
    lawyers 89; positivist philosophy
    89–90
Final Funding Agreement James Hardie
    case study 45
Finn, P. 10–11, 88–9
Flood, J. 9, 28
Foley, T. 113
Foundations of the Metaphysics of
    Morals, Kant 73
Fried, C. 62–3
future tort claimants 21, 43, 44, 108

Giannarelli v Wraith 60
global financial crisis (2008) 2,
    14, 90
Godinho, C. 15
Grace, D. 79

Haigh, G. 27–8, 35, 42
Hart, H. L. A. 54–5
Hersh, R. 105
Hinchly, V. 15, 17, 47
home renovators 21, 45
honesty 9, 11, 12, 68, 77, 79, 81, 82,
    87, 90, 97, 102, 108, 109, 120
Hospital Products Ltd v United States
    Surgical Corporation 11
Hutchinson, A. 85, 105, 112, 123
hyper-rationality of lawyers 103

in-house corporate lawyers 15–16
intellectual virtues 71–2, 76, 81, 82,
    97, 104

Jackson, D. 22, 27–8, 30–1, 38–40,
    43–4, 64–5, 109–10
Jackson Inquiry 20, 44 *see* New
    South Wales (Australia), Special
    Commission of Inquiry into the
    Medical Research and Compensation
    Foundation (Report 2004) Jackson,
    D. Commissioner
Jackson Report 20, 45
James Hardie & Co Pty Ltd v Hall as
    Administrator of Estate of Putt 24
James Hardie (JH) 20; calculating
    tort liability 21–3; external lawyers
    and restructure 27–32; legal entity
    separation 23–5; new funding
    arrangement 44–5; US Business
    25–6
James Hardie group (JH group) 47,
    107; James Hardie and Co Pty Ltd
    24; liabilities of 45
James Hardie Industries Limited
    (JHIL) 2, 4, 20, 45–6, 63, 78, 91,
    107, 118, 119; announcement by
    84; asbestos tort liability 20–6;
    ASX disclosure obligation 32–6;
    court approval of restructure 36–41;
    external lawyers 35–6, 83; external
    lawyers and restructure 27–32;
    MRCF funding shortfall 41–3; new
    funding arrangement 44–5; positivist
    and moral philosophies in 83–4,
    87–8, 94–5; and positivist TLE 63–6;
    restructure and best interests 30–2
James Hardie Industries NV (JHI NV)
    30, 37, 41, 65
James Hardie Industries NV,
    Explanatory Memorandum 38, 111
James Hardie Industries NV v
    Australian Securities Investments
    Commission 34
James Hardie's lawyers: applying
    new model of legal ethics 107; core
    principles of new model 107–8;
    moral reasoning 109–12; moral
    sensitivity 108–9; practical wisdom
    109–12
Johns-Manville Corporation, US 23
justice 8–9, 58, 64; administration of
    84, 85, 89; Aristotelian philosophy
    of 86–8, 120; as central normative

touchstone 52; Kantian philosophy
of 87, 88; lawyers' duties to 2, 3,
6, 9, 51, 52, 60, 78, 84, 105, 109,
114, 120; lawyers' professional
obligations to 85; positivist
philosophy 85–6

Kantian philosophy 68–9, 73, 105,
120–1; decision-making process 76;
fiduciary and confidentiality duties
91; importance of reason 73–4;
lawyers' knowledge in 121; moral
duties 74–6; practical wisdom 93–4;
professional integrity for lawyers 82;
universal moral laws and categorical
imperative 74; *see also* Aristotelian
philosophy
Kingsford Smith, D. 8–9, 16, 19
knowledge 68, 70, 92; in applied
Aristotelian and Kantian
philosophies 121; of behavioural
science 98; of ethical principles 58;
of law and legal duties 103; lawyers'
excellence in 124
Kohlberg, L. 105
Kronman, A. 93
Kruse, K. 48–9, 56

Law Society of NSW (Australia);
Statement of Ethics 12
lawyers: asserting lawyers'
professional independence
114–15; behavioural ethics 13;
confidentiality duties 88–91;
corporate 14–19, 99; duties to law
and justice 84–8; ethics in lawyers'
advice 57–60; expertise in law
and justice 8, 68; fiduciary duties
88–91, 120; good character of 70,
79–82, 93; moral reasoning 104–6,
109–11; moral sensitivity 108–9;
practical wisdom and judgement
91–5, 104–6, 109–12; professional
bodies 124; professional duties
and TLE 2, 31, 51–2, 60–1, 120;
professional independence 7–8, 98;
professional integrity for 78–84;
professional obligations 4, 6–13,
117; psychological issues for 2;
role as moral agents 50–1; role as

political agents 48–50; statutory
legal ethics obligation 18; *see also*
James Hardie's lawyers
lawyer-to-client relationship 59;
consequence of positivist TLE 108;
principle of clients' loyalty and 86;
role of Kantian duties and moral
laws in 105; and TLE 78
lawyer-to-client relationship between
Allens and JHIL 20, 28, 45–6; court
approval of JHIL's restructure 36–41;
external lawyers and restructure
27–32; James Hardie's asbestos tort
liability 20–6; James Hardie's new
funding arrangement 44–5; JHIL's
ASX disclosure obligation 32–6;
MRCF funding shortfall 41–3
legal compliance 65–6, 86
legal entity separation 23–5
legal ethics 1, 7, 11, 96; across lawyers'
professional obligations, codes, and
statute 19; Aristotelian philosophies
as 124; empirical studies in UK
17; Kantian moral principles in 87,
124; professional bodies' statement
of 12–13; *see also* new legal ethics
model; statutory legal ethics;
theoretical legal ethics (TLE)
legal imagination 114
legal obligation of lawyers 12, 15, 46,
47, 58, 63, 83, 99
legal practice 9, 18, 79, 82; applying
new moral TLE model in 2; client
supremacy and 61–3; cognitive
processes and 98–101; ethical issues
in 19, 46; ethics role in 56–7; legal
ethics and 118–19; role of principles
of TLE 4; *see also* theoretical legal
ethics (TLE)
*Legal Profession Uniform Law Act
(NSW) Australia* 7
legal validity 55
Lewis, P. 60
Luban, D. 48, 50, 56, 58, 79, 81, 86,
91, 120

Macaulay, M. 79, 82
Macdonald, P. 31, 33, 39, 42
Marchesi v Barnes 34
Mason, J. 11, 60

Medical Research and Compensation
Foundation (MRCF) 26, 64,
87–8, 107; adequacy of funding 27;
funding 39, 64; funding shortfall
41–3; JHIL's allocation to 30; JHIL's
external lawyers and 42–3
mesothelioma 21, 22, 45
Mill, J. S. 68
Moorhead, R. 10, 15, 17, 47, 118
moral accountability: new model of
legal ethics 97
moral agents, lawyers' role as 50–1
moral duties: duty of honesty 74–5;
duty of respect 76; duty to help
others 75
moral imagination 98, 106, 114, 121
moral integrity 105
morality 53, 55; of actions to advance
client causes 65; of client's cause
64–5; ordinary 48, 50, 54, 58, 80;
see also role morality
moral neutrality 54, 64; morality of
actions to advance client causes 65;
morality of client's cause 64–5
moral non-accountability, positivist
TLE 54
moral partiality 66
moral philosophy 68–9, 120–1; of
Aristotelian philosophy 68–73, 81–2,
124; of Kantian philosophy 73–6, 82,
124; in Re James Hardie 83–8, 94–5
moral principles 48, 67, 68
moral reasoning 97, 103, 109, 121;
enhancing 104; lawyers 104–6,
109–11
moral rightness 86, 87, 120
moral sensitivity 96, 97, 101–3, 121;
lawyers and 108–9, 112; positivist
TLE's absence of 111
moral virtue 71–2, 82, 91, 93, 97, 102
Morley v Australian Securities and
Investments Commission 33, 35
Murphy, J. 92, 103

neutrality principle 90
new legal ethics model: originality
of 121–2; significance of 122–4;
see also legal ethics
new moral theoretical legal ethics
(TLE) model 2–3, 8, 12, 30, 96;

core principles 96–7; steps in 97–8;
see also moral non-accountability,
positivist TLE
New South Wales (Australia), Special
Commission of Inquiry into the
Medical Research and Compensation
Foundation (Report 2004) Jackson,
D. Commissioner 19
Nicolson, D. 11
non-accountability 54, 66

Oakley, E. 17, 49–50

Parker, C. 16, 18, 30, 52, 84–5;
partisanship principle *see* principle
of partisanship
partly paid shares 37; cancellation of
38–9, 41, 42, 95, 110; issue in JHIL
107; JHIL's strategy regarding 109;
JHI NV's 65
Pepper, S. L. 58–9, 73, 92–3
political agents, lawyers' role as 48–50
positivist philosophy 66, 80–1;
fiduciary and confidentiality
duties 89–90; lawyers' duties to
law and justice 85–6; practical
wisdom 92
positivist theoretical legal ethics (TLE)
1, 4, 9, 16–17, 47, 62–6, 81, 83, 96,
111, 119; failure of 2; importance of
deleterious effects 4, 5, 52; principles
48, 56, 61; problems with 1; role
morality 49; supporters 119; *see also*
new moral theoretical legal ethics
(TLE) model; theoretical legal ethics
(TLE)
'power and vulnerability' principle 11
practical wisdom 72–3, 78, 96, 97, 103,
109, 121; Aristotelian philosophy
92–3; Kantian philosophy 93–4;
lawyers and 92, 104–6, 111; moral
philosophies 94–5; positivist
philosophy 92, 94–5
principle: of accountability 97; of
justice 86, 120; of morality 97; of
neutrality 54; of non-accountability
54; of universalisation 74
principle of partisanship 54, 63,
86, 89; advancing client, JHIL's,
interests within law 63–4; justice

and public good 64; professional
independence 64
professional autonomy 7, 60, 61
professional bodies' statement of ethics
12–13
professional integrity for lawyers 78–9,
97, 105–6; acts of 120; Aristotelian
philosophy and 81–2; importance of
integrity for legal profession 79–80;
Kantian philosophy and 82; positivist
and moral philosophies in Re James
Hardie 83–4; positivist philosophy
and 80–1; primary obligation of 96
professional obligations of lawyers 6,
68, 78, 109, 111–12
prudence 72–3, 92–3
public good 3, 5, 6, 10, 64, 115, 122

Ramsay, I. 29, 37
rational choices 71, 72, 76
rationality 68
Redmond, P. 31, 42
reflective thinking 99, 104
Rhode, D. 10, 59, 62, 80, 123
Robb, D. 27
Robinson, A. A. 20
Rogers, J. 8–9, 16, 19
role morality: lawyers' 48, 50, 51;
positivist 49–51
Rondel v Worsley 85

Salomon v Salomon & Co Ltd 14
Salz A, and Collins, R, An Independent
Review of Barclays 'Business
Practices' (Salz Review): Report
2013 53
Santow, J. 37–41, 65, 110
self-perception 13
Shafron, P. 22, 27, 31, 33–5, 39
Shafron v Australian Securities and
Investments Commission 35
Sharot, T. 100
Simon, W. 3, 50, 52, 55, 60, 81
solicitors 12–13, 20, 31
Solicitors Regulatory Authority (SRA)
UK, Solicitors' Independence,
Report 14, 17n90, 18–19
Solicitors Regulatory Authority,
(SRA) UK, Statement A: Ethics
Professionalism and Judgement 17

Solomon, R. 77
Spender, P. 23–4
Spirit of the law, Barclays Bank, Salz
Review 53
statutory duty of care 23, 28, 33
statutory legal ethics 12, 49; *see also*
theoretical legal ethics (TLE)
stress of handling multiple client
files 100
substantive legal reasoning 105
surplus funds 32

Tenbrunsel, A. 98–100, 105
theoretical legal ethics (TLE) 1, 3,
6, 12, 21, 47, 68, 78, 117; client
supremacy 60–3; James Hardie
case and positivist TLE 63–6; law
and ethics 53–60; lawyers 48–52;
principles 4; *see also* new moral
theoretical legal ethics (TLE) model
time pressure of deadlines for
lawyers 100
tort liabilities 64; asbestos 22–3;
funding for 63; and restructure 27–8
tort victims 21, 29, 31, 32, 43,
46, 63, 83; demand of funding
arrangement for 43; funds in MRCF
for 94; protection for 65, 94, 107;
stakeholder 94
Trade Practices Act 41
Trowbridge Deloitte Limited
(Trowbridge) 21, 31–2; report 22,
27, 31, 36, 42
trustworthiness 79, 90

unethical decisions of client 12, 57, 99,
100, 114, 122
universalisation 74, 104
universality 94
universal moral laws 69, 73, 74, 87, 95,
104, 105, 110
Urmson, J. 70–1, 92–3
utilitarian ethics 68
utilitarian philosophy 69

Van Hooft, S. 81
Vaughan, S. 14, 15, 17, 19, 49–50
virtue ethics 68–70
virtues 71, 102; and excellence
71; intellectual 71–2, 76, 81, 82,

97, 104; moral 71–2, 82, 91, 93, 97, 102
Vischer, R. K. 4, 59–60, 106, 119

Wasserstrom, R. 47, 50–2, 54, 118
Webb, J. 11

Weber, M. 6, 120
Wendel, B. 48–9, 51–5, 57–61
Wilkins, D. 84

Zimmermann, A. 7, 47, 53

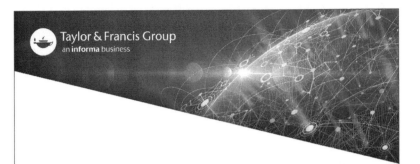

Printed and bound by CPI Group (UK) Ltd, Croydon, CR0 4YY

11/04/2025

01844012-0007